The Mensa® Genius Quiz-a-Day Book

Other Books by Dr. Abbie F. Salny
and the Members of Mensa

with Marvin Grosswirth

The Mensa Genius Quiz Book
The Mensa Genius Quiz Book 2

with Lewis Burke Frumkes

The Mensa Think-Smart Book

The Mensa Book of Words, Word Games,
    Puzzles, and Oddities

The MENSA® Genius
Quiz-a-Day Book

Dr. Abbie F. Salny
and the Members of Mensa

Addison-Wesley Publishing Company
Reading, Massachusetts   Menlo Park, California   New York
Don Mills, Ontario   Wokingham, England   Amsterdam   Bonn
Sidney   Singapore   Tokyo   Madrid   San Juan   Paris
Seoul   Milan   Mexico City   Taipei

To Jerry, as always

Many of the designations used by manufacturers and sellers to distinguish their products are claimed as trademarks. Where those designations appear in this book and Addison-Wesley was aware of a trademark claim, the designations have been printed in initial capital letters (e.g., Mensa).

MENSA is a registered trademark and service mark of American Mensa, Ltd. It is used in this book with the permission of American Mensa, Ltd.

Library of Congress Cataloging-in-Publication Data

Salny, Abbie F.
  The Mensa genius quiz-a-day book / Abbie F. Salny and the members of Mensa.
      p.   cm.
    ISBN 0-201-13549-3
    1. Puzzles.   2. Literary recreations.   3. Mensa.
I. Mensa.   II. Title.
GV1493.S247   1989
793.73—dc20   89-14942

Cover design by Hannus Design Associates
Text design by Joyce C. Westc
Set in 10-point Century Schoolbook by Compset Inc., Beverly, MA

8 9 10 11 12–DO–96959493
Eighth printing, July 1993

Acknowledgments

Special thanks to Mensans Bob Buethe, Ron Frederick, Friend Kierstead, Ron Ruemmler, Marilyn Seltzer, and Russ Washburne. They corrected, annotated, criticized, and helped. Thanks also to Lucille Hitchuk and Gene Sheridan for their clerical assistance.

The following list includes those Mensans who helped by taking the various puzzles included in this book. Not all did every puzzle, of course, but I'm grateful to everyone. My apologies to anyone whose name does not appear. I could not read, or find, a few names on the answer sheets. If you will send me your name now, we'll include it in a later printing.

Lois Abel
Charles E. Adams
Micki Ross Adams
Virginia Andrews
N.B. Angelo
Suzanne Armstrong
Warner Ashby
Jean Babcock
John E. Ballinger
Pat Bechlear

Carol Bell-Jesion
Paul Berghold
Jerome Bernstein
Mervin Bierman
H.W. Bodley
W.E. Bowser
Joan K. Boyer
M. Brockhoff
Lorin Browning
Robert A. Buethe

Jerri Burket
Jerry Butler
Shanna Cartwright
Paul D. Cernota
Terri A. Chepregi
Laurence P. Ching
W. Edward Christiansen, Jr.
Elizabeth Claire
Lorilyn Coggins
Seth Cohen
Roy Cornelius
George M. Couch
Joel Cox
Antonia Dailey
Jane Dalton
Evelyn N. Doody
Pat Doody
Judy Dosse
Amby Duncan-Carr
Wendy Ebersberger
Leslie A. Ellis
Sean M. Ferrell
Leslie Fife
Marian Fox
Ron Frederick
Sonia Follett Fuller
Henry Gertzman
R.O. Ginsburg
Vella L. Goebel
Larry Gomberg
Al Greengold
Yale L. Greenspoon
Elaine Gruber
Michael Hanson

Monroe Harden
Patricia A. Hardesty
Charles Harding
Amy Harold
Thomas Henneman
Porter Henry
Dayle Hodge
Jack Howell
Michael Jankowski
Jerry Javine
Bruce W. Jean
Elvin Jensen
John M. Jensen
Kathy Jones
Donna Jones-Cosgrove
Arielle Kagan
Kevin Kauffman
Ted Kelly
Mary Lee Kemper
Friend H. Kierstead, Jr.
Virginia Krenn
Ravi Krishnan
Florence Kuehn
Teri Lacher
Nancy Laine
Eileen Leskovec
Rich Loeffler
Virginia Long
Gene Lucas
M.P. Ludlum
Melinda Maidens
Ward Mardfin
Teresa MarQuand

Stuart Maudlin
Lois McDonley
Vernon McFarlin
Ernest McLain
Barbara H. Miller
Phyllis Miller
Jean Moffett
Caroline Monks
Barbara A. Moore
Dennis B. Moore
Mildred Morgan and family
Rosalie Moscovitch
Kathy Mullholland
Warren Murphy
Diane Nagel
Edward J. Nasipak
Caryn Neumann
Everett Newton
Ruby V. North
Kathleen E. O'Malley
Florence Otis
D. June Owen
Howard S. Passel
Kyle J. Perun
Thomas M. Phelps
Sharon Pidgeon
Heather L. Preston
Dimitri Raftopolous
Bill Raiford
Gloria Reiser
Kate Retzlaff
Cecilia M. Roberts
Mary Lou Robinson

Wm. Ridgway, Jr.
Mary Lou Robinson
Diane Rozek
Pat Rudy-Baese
Ron Ruemmler
Charlie Runtz
Minerva A. Russell
Vicki P. Samples
Danika Lea Sanders
Jules Savan
Sharon Scanlin
Kenneth Schwartz
Marilyn Seltzer
Dave Senner
Terri Shaw
Kenneth M. Silver
William M. Sloane
Donald J. Strand
Ray Suhles
Merrilee Tanner
Colleen J. Theusch
Elaine Thompson
Hank Trent
N. Trigobotti
Barbara R. Tysinger
Tony C. Vaca
Alden Vaitulis
Stanley Veyitl
Alice Volkert
Roger Volkert
Charles R. Voracek
Mary Washburn
Russ Washburne

Shirley Washburne
G.H. Waxter
A. Weiss
Frank Wershing
Hugh White and family
Ray Wilbur

Sherie J. Winslow
Cynthia Wolford
Jeanne R. Wood
Mark A. Yezzi
Joe Zanca
Carl Zimmerman

Contents

To the Reader

This puzzle book is intended to amuse, edify, instruct, but mostly to interest you, the clever reader. The puzzles have been tested on several hundred Mensa members, who racked their brains on the more difficult questions or sneered at what look like easy questions. But be warned! There are tricks in some of the apparently easy puzzles, and even the Mensa members, in many instances, failed to spot the hidden traps.

The puzzles are arranged in chronological order over the course of the year—one for each day and an extra one for Leap Years. The answers can be found in the back of the book, organized by date: the answers for the first day of each month, then the answers for the second day, and so on to the thirty-first. The percentage of Mensa members who solved that puzzle correctly is given with every answer. Most of these percentages have been rounded off to the nearest 5 percent for the sake of convenience.

You may find some old puzzles in new guises. You may find others that are totally new to you. There's even one type of puzzle in this book that I invented myself (see February 8). All the rest were inspired by puzzles that people have been making since one person first passed on the "Riddle of the Sphinx" to another. Magic squares are thousands of years old; number puzzles have existed since the early days of written numbers; paradoxes and logic puzzles were recorded by the early Greeks. Word ladders and alphametics are more recent, having been invented by Lewis Carroll and A. H. Hunter within the last two hundred years. But there is little new under the sun.

One thing which is not new is alternate answers. Try as a puzzle author might, unless a puzzle is the type to which only one answer can possibly be given, there may well be alternate solutions. If you find a clever, more elegant, or more interesting solution, please drop me a note. I'd be glad to hear from you.

All the puzzles were proofed by my nitpicking husband, Jerome Salny, but all errors are my sole responsibility. Happy puzzling!

Abbie F. Salny

What Is Mensa?

First of all, Mensa is not an acronym. It is the Latin word meaning "table," and it indicates that all members are equal. (Remember King Arthur's Round Table?) Of course, some are more equal than others, because those who become involved and participate in the multitude of activities Mensa offers get the most from the society. The sole requirement for membership in Mensa is a score in the top 2 percent of the population on any standard intelligence test or the equivalent (130 on the Wechsler scale, 132 on the Stanford-Binet, 1250 on the Scholastic Aptitude Test after 1977).

Because this is the only criterion for membership, the diversity of human beings in Mensa is immense. Members include authors, executives, carpenters, dancers, physicists, students, and many other kinds of people. You can well imagine the interest and fun generated when Mensans get together at a gathering (the official term). The talk can range over all and any subjects. One has the pleasure of hearing from an intelligent expert in a field other than one's own. There is the delight in recognizing a new idea, a new concept, or a new outlook on an old theme. And there is just plain fun. Mensans love to play games of all kinds—computer games, word games, logic games, silly games. Most groups have a Games Night when those so inclined to this sort of thing (the sort of thing in this book) can participate.

Mensans band together in Special Interest Groups (SIGs) of members with a common fascination or desire. These interests run from the Age of Chivalry SIG to the Feudal Japan SIG, the Scripophily (paper money) SIG, the Skydiving SIG, through M.A.R.I.A.N., a SIG devoted to nurturing and visiting, in person or by letter, the sick and dying, and to the Vacation Network SIG and the Singles Network SIG.

Many Mensans participate in the society exclusively by mail. They get their local newsletter telling them what is going on in their area; they receive the Mensa Bulletin and the *International Journal,* which tell them about national and international Mensa; and they may belong to a SIG which, though it may never meet, ties hundreds of Mensans together in a postal network.

Who are these Mensans, anyway? Mensans tend to be reasonably well educated, but we have plenty of high school dropouts as well as Ph.D.'s. Mensans tend to have above-average incomes—but many do not, preferring to spend their time on avocations of consuming interest. Mensans tend to have a slightly smaller number of children than the national average—but we have a highly active Gifted Children's Program, with a national network of coordinators. The society also publishes a newsletter full of ideas for gifted children. Mensans tend to be ages thirty or over, but there is a very active Young Mensa for people who are twenty-two or younger. Mensans tend to be verbal and fluent, whether on paper or in person. We talk and talk—but we listen, too.

Mensans are just like everyone else, but more so. You meet a lot of intense people in Mensa who throw themselves wholeheartedly into what they do for the society. (All Mensa activity is volunteer and unpaid, except for a small staff at national headquarters in Brooklyn.) Many members help out with the intellectual and scientific activities of the Mensa Education and Research Foundation (MERF). This branch runs the numerous scholarships (to which this book contributes), the *Mensa Research Journal,* the surveys, the Awards for Excellence, and all the other activities that satisfy our intellectual side. MERF raises money for special projects and is limited only by what we can raise and the vision of those who propose projects. MERF also collaborates on the intellectual Colloquium. It is the idealistic, social-service side of Mensa, and contributions to MERF are tax deductible.

But above all, Mensa is friends. Whether in the local chapter or in any of the thirty countries around the world where Mensa exists, it means finding ready-made friends. There is even a group organized to provide hospitality wherever in the world (almost) you might travel. You need to have had the experience of arriving by plane in a strange land at midnight, tired and droopy, to be welcomed by Mensa strangers-who-will-soon-be-friends, to realize what this means.

And that's meeting one or two Mensans at a time. There are large gatherings of anywhere from seventy-five to fifteen hundred Mensans. The joint American-Canadian Annual Gathering at Montreal in 1988 was attended by fifteen hundred Mensans from both countries. For many, it was like being in a room filled with bubbly champagne, full of friendship and good cheer. What did the Mensans do at this gathering? They talked; they took French lessons; they attended lectures on mathematics, on art, on history, on romance, on Montreal; they talked; they ate at the hotel banquets and nibbled in the Mensa hospitality suites, which are always jammed wall to wall with talkers; they went on sightseeing tours; they went to a French-Canadian sugar shack for a party; they talked; and when they finished with all these activities, they talked some more.

There are many such gatherings a year. There are even gathering addicts, who spend their vacations visiting one regional gathering after another, each with its own special flavor, or attending the Colloquium, a biannual event sponsored by both MERF and Mensa with meetings devoted to intellectual topics and renowned speakers. Past themes have included "The Future," "The Arts," and "Man and Science."

Mensa is fun, it is serious, it is intellectually stimulating, it is friendly. In short, Mensa is the sum of fifty-odd thousand bright people, effervescing.

January

The calendar as we know it is the result of a great deal of work by the Romans. Even the word *calendar* derives from the Latin *kalends,* a system of reckoning.

The Roman calendar originally started with what we now call March, which had 31 days, followed by April (30 days), May (31), June (29), Quintilis (31), Sextilis (29), September (29), October (31), November and December (29 each). There were a good many extra days in this system, and January and February appeared more or less at whim. This calendar became a political football when the pontifex maximus, the highest priest of Roman religion, was given the power to regulate the empty dates. By extending or shortening the final periods, for example, an unpopular politician could be pushed out of office early, or a popular one kept in long past his elected term. By the time of Julius Caesar, January was falling in the fall, and the entire system was obviously in need of a major overhaul.

Caesar enlisted the aid of astronomers and set up a system much like that of the ancient Egyptians, who had the year figured out to within a few hours. During 46 B.C., the 445-day "Year of Confusion," Caesar added days, made January and February settled months, and gave every fourth February an extra day for Leap Year.

January 1

Janus was the Roman god who was represented with two bearded heads placed back to back so that he could look forward and backward at the same time. A palindrome is a word, phrase, or sentence that reads the same forward and backward, so it seems especially appropriate for Janus's month, January. Try to come up with palindromes from the following clues, in which the word division is given. (Example: First man introduces himself to first woman—Madam, I'm Adam.)

Query by rodent-phobic person:

— — —　　— —　　—　　— — —　　—

— — — ?

Comment by cake- and pie-loving overweight person about meal habits:

— — — — — — — —　　—

— — — — — — — — .

January 2

At my favorite fruit stand in Puzzleland, an orange costs 18¢, a pineapple costs 27¢, and a grape costs 15¢. Using the same logic, can you tell how much a mango costs?

January 3

Even if you don't like cats, you should be able to determine the following words. Each of these includes the word CAT. (Example: grape—mus*cat*)

A dreadful event:

— — — — — — — — — — —

A robber who climbs walls:

— — —   — — — — — —

A systematized list:

— — — — — — — — —

January 4

Margot likes knights but not battlers; she likes writing but not typing; she likes to listen but not to sing. Does she like an unknown or a famous author?

January 5

My husband and I can't seem to get our watches to work properly. His consistently runs one minute per hour fast, and mine runs two minutes per hour slow. This morning we nearly missed a wedding because our watches were an hour apart and we looked at the slower one. How many hours had elapsed since we set both of them properly?

January 6

Cressida didn't like to tell her age, so when she was asked, her mother answered for her. Her mother said, "I'm just seven times as old as she is now. In twenty years, she'll be just half the age that I will be then." How old is clever little Cressida?

January 7

This type of puzzle used to be very popular among puzzlers who thought they were poets, and poets who thought they were puzzlers. The verse spells out a word letter by letter, and often defines that word as well. "My first" refers to the word's first letter, and so on. Can you discover the word that this verse describes?

> My first is in fish but not in snail
> My second in rabbit but not in tail
> My third in up but not in down
> My fourth in tiara not in crown
> My fifth in tree you plainly see
> My whole a food for you and me

January 8

All the vowels (A, E, I, O, and U, but not Y) have been removed from the following proverb, and the remaining letters broken into groups of three letters each. Replace the vowels to find the proverb.

BRD   SFF   THR   FLC   KTG   THR.

January 9

One letter—a different letter for each word—has been removed from each of the following words. At least three of that letter are missing in each one. Replace the missing letters to find the words.

ILIN   HAERAN   ILLOARE

January 10

What is the four-digit number in which the first digit is one-third the second, the third is the sum of the first and second, and the last is three times the second?

January 11

If six winkles and three wonkles cost 15¢, and you can buy nine wonkles and three winkles for the same 15¢, what will it cost to buy one hundred wonkles?

January 12

The names of three famous cheeses are "interlettered" in the following line. All the letters are in the correct order for each word. Unscramble your cheeses:

R L C O I M H Q B E U U D E R D F O G E R R A T R

January 13

The same seven letters, if rearranged, will make two different words. These words will make the following sentences (more or less) complete. Fill in the missing letters.

The job they were doing was long and
— — — — — — — . Every few hours,
the workmen put down their tools to go
— — — — — — — .

January 14

It's hard to go back to school after vacation, but you have to get to work sometime. Go from FAIL to PASS in only four steps, changing one letter at a time and making a good English word at each step.

F   A   I   L

—   —   —   —

—   —   —   —

—   —   —   —

P   A   S   S

January 15

Since it is January, thoughts often turn, fondly or not, to snowflakes. Each shape of snowflake in the boxes below has a numerical value. The sum of each line and column has been given for all but one line. Fill in the missing sum.

❄	❄	☆	✳	**?**
❄	✽	☆	✽	**85**
✳	☆	❄	✳	**87**
✽	✳	☆	✳	**82**
87	**86**	**93**	**79**	

January 16

Rearrange these six matchsticks to make "nothing." No matchsticks may be bent, broken, or placed over each other.

January 17

This simple substitution cryptogram is a warning. (A substitution cryptogram is one in which each letter is replaced by another letter, number, or symbol; CAT becomes DBU when the next letter of the alphabet is used.) Can you solve the cipher?

        S V   D S L   R H   G L L
        H S Z I K   H L N V G R N V H
        X F G H   S R N H V O U .

January 18

Using all the digits from 1 to 9, you can construct many different additions (for example, $317 + 628 = 945$). There are four such examples which have a total of 468. Find the missing numbers. You *may not* simply reverse the top and bottom numbers; new combinations must be found.

	1 x x	x x 5	x 9 x	x x x
	x x x	x x x	x x x	x 7 x
	4 6 8	4 6 8	4 6 8	4 6 8

January 19

How many common English words can you make from the letters DRIBA? Use all the letters each time.

January 20

You have decided to take your morning run in preparation for the local marathon at an average speed of 6 miles per hour. Unfortunately, you are not in as good shape as you thought, and you are running uphill. You find that you complete a half of the run, all uphill, at an average speed of only 3 miles per hour. How fast must you run to make the return trip—all downhill—at an average speed for the entire round trip of 6 miles per hour?

January 21

In that same marathon, which you watched from the side-walk, Sam was faster than Jack. Denise beat Jim, but lost to Jack. Who came in last?

January 22

After paying all your holiday bills, you're very short of cash. You have a total of $9.60 in your pocket. The money is composed of equal numbers of quarters, dimes, and nickels, but no other coins. How many of each of those three coins do you have?

January 23

Each of the following words except one can be rearranged to spell the name of a person or city. Unscramble the words to find the one that cannot be unscrambled. Both parts must be done correctly for full credit.

ANIMAL   BUTCHERS   PASTURE
PANELS   VIKING

January 24

Here are two more palindromes—phrases reading the same in both directions (Madam, I'm Adam). Word division is given for each.

Consumed a Greek delicacy:

— — —   — — — —

Where Napoleon dined:

— — — —   — — — — —

January 25

Entire countries are hidden in the sentences below—at least their names are. One or more names appear in each statement. Find the countries.

Don't reach in a crack in the rocks, there might be snakes there.

While I was on the highway called the Alcan, a daily occurrence was car breakdown.

The top social class, as defined by many investigators, is the upper-upper.

January 26

Harper and Rose Lee were debating the major purchase of some candy. They found out, by looking at the prices, that they could get three tiny bags of jellybeans and two tiny bags of chocolate chips for 24¢, which was under their limit of a quarter. They could also get four tiny bags of chocolates and two tiny bags of jellybeans for the same 24¢. How much did each tiny bag of chocolates cost?

January 27

The following quotation, from a famous author born on this date in 1832, has had all its vowels removed and has been broken into groups of three letters. (There's one null letter at the end.) Put back the vowels to read the quotation.

THT	MHS	CMT	HWL	RSS	DTT
LKF	MNY	THN	GSF	SHS	NDS
HPS	NDS	LNG	WXF	CBB	GSN
DKN	GSX.				

January 28

The following coiled sentence contains an idea that every motorist agrees with. Start at the right spot and move, letter by letter, in any direction to find the sentence.

```
V   E   O   E   T
E   U   Y   L   P
R   Y   S   L   A
H   T   R   O   M
I   N   A   A   D
G   E   X   R   T
E   C   O   E   I
P   O   T   F   D
T   H   W   O   L
```

January 29

One letter can replace the first letter of each word pair shown below so that two new English words are formed. Place the letter you have used for both words on the line between the words. (Example: RAIN _____ DARK = MAIN __M__ MARK). When you have finished, the new letters will spell out a new English word.

MAIL	_____	PINK
CART	_____	SAID
GRID	_____	RIMLESS
LINK	_____	BOUND
ROWED	_____	RIPPLE

January 30

At the top below is a box that has been unfolded. Next to it are six folded boxes. Which of these folded boxes *cannot* be made from the unfolded box? (There may be more than one.)

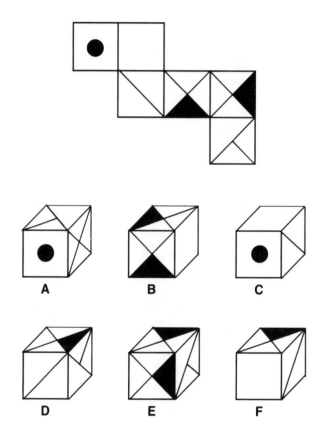

January 31

Each of the following words includes the letters JAN in order. (They may contain another J or A or N, which does not appear in the lines shown.) The definition for each word is given. Find the words.

A variety of semiprecious stone, a color either blue
 or orangy: J A __ __ N __ __
A type of soldier: J A N __ __ __ __ __ __
Pertaining, now, to the Democratic party of the U.S.,
 but originally with a slightly different meaning.
 Adjectival form of politician's name:
                         J __ __ __ __ __ __ __ __ __ A N

February

Because February fell at the end of the Roman year, it was assigned fewer days than the rest of the months. According to legends, Julius Caesar and Augustus each took one day from February to add to the month named after him. They seem to have covered their thefts successfully, however, as these legends cannot be verified.

If you think cold February days are hard now, you would not have liked being around a few centuries ago. Average temperatures in Europe dropped during the thirteenth century, and they remained lower than they are now through the 1700s. The Vikings had to abandon their settlement on Greenland when this "Little Ice Age" began. Canals in Holland froze. The wine industry in England, which had flourished under the Romans, disappeared.

In London, February often produced a "Frost Fair" on the Thames. The river was frozen so solid for several weeks that a whole country fair could be held on the ice. We are indebted to English diary keepers and writers for our knowledge of this lost tradition. The last such fair occurred in 1814, the approximate beginning date of the current warming trend.

February 1

A palindrome is a word or phrase that reads the same backward as forward, such as "Madam, I'm Adam." The following two palindromes are more difficult, but not impossible. Word divisions are shown:

> A zookeeper announces that he has captured two fewer than a dozen beasts by hitting them hard with a reticulated object and putting them inside it.

— — —   — — — — — —   —

— — — —   — —   —   — — — .

Spoiled children of performing luminaries:

— — — —   — — — — —

February 2

The following puzzle consists of a proverb with all its vowels removed. The remaining letters have been broken into groups of four. Put back the vowels to find the proverb.

FLND   HSMN   YRSN   PRTD.

February 3

The coiled sentence below will complete a rhyme with the first line "Murphy's Law is very fine." Move from the correct starting letter in any direction, letter by letter.

```
T K K O E
I E C F N
P E E F I
S Y N T L
O U R H E
```

February 4

You can often place a word between a pair of other words to form an entirely new word or phrase with each of them (example: SCHOOL *BOOK* BAG). In fact, one four-letter word will fit in all three pairs below. What is it?

BACK	____	SOME
LEFT	____	WORK
FORE	____	SHAKE

February 5

If six puzzle makers can compose nine puzzles in a day and a half, how many puzzle makers does it take to compose 270 puzzles in thirty days?

February 6

It is nice in real life, but it's much easier on paper. Can you go from POOR to RICH in seven steps, changing one letter at a time, and making a good English word each time? (There are several solutions.)

P	O	O	R
—	—	—	—
—	—	—	—
—	—	—	—
—	—	—	—
—	—	—	—
—	—	—	—
R	I	C	H

February 7

Two youngsters were running as hard as they could. They averaged 6 miles per hour, and then had to rest. On the way back, they averaged only 4 miles per hour for the same distance. Not counting resting time, what was their average speed?

February 8

If Brazil is east of New York, cross out all the W's and X's. If not, cross out all the A's. If Henry VIII lived in the same century as Columbus, cross out all the Y's. If not, cross out the M's and N's. If Golden Gate Bridge is the longest suspension bridge in the world, cross out all the S's and E's. If not, cross out all the I's and Z's. What word do you have left?

M X Y E Z W N X Y Z S I I X Y A Z W X I

February 9

The following addition example uses letters instead of numbers. Each letter must be replaced with a number—the same number each time the letter appears. The puzzle will then be correct mathematically.

$$
\begin{array}{r}
OH \\
OH \\
OH \\
\underline{OH} \\
NO!
\end{array}
$$

February 10

All the vowels have been removed from a popular proverb and the remaining letters broken up into groups of four (with three nulls). Replace the vowels to read the proverb.

LLTH   TGLT   TRSS   NTGL   DXXX

February 11

Each of the following words contains the letters FEB. Fill in the missing letters. (Additional F, E, B letters may appear but not be shown.)

Feverish: F E B _ _ _ _

Untenable; that cannot be excused or justified:

                      _ _ _ _ F E _ _ _ B _ _

Not strong: F E _ B _ _

February 12

You've had a tough time lately. Birthdays, weddings, what-all, have just about brought your finances down to your household piggy bank. With your trusty broad blade knife, you manage to extract quite a few coins, for a total of $16. To your surprise, you have exactly the same number of half dollars, quarters, and nickels. How many of each do you have?

February 13

If Susan is 10, Arabella is 20, and Jim and Neal are both 5, but Richard is 10, how much is Jennifer by the same system?

February 14

Valentine's Day has its roots in the tradition that Saint Valentine provided dowries for unmarried poor girls. His feast day thus became a celebration of love and marriage, and young men sent tokens of affection to young women of their choice. Now Valentine's Day seems to have gotten a little out of hand, with people sending wishes to their mothers-in-law, aunts, teachers, all their third-grade classmates, and many others. Given this crush of cards, if seven valentine makers can make seven valentines in one hour and forty minutes, how long does it take fourteen valentine makers to make fourteen valentines?

February 15

The office team is out racing at the skating rink during a long lunch hour. Samantha beat Jim. Louise was not last. Dennis was beaten by Jack and Louise, in that order. Jim was not first. Jack lost to Jim. Who won?

February 16

How many common English words can you make from the letters AEKL? (All the letters must be used for each word.)

February 17

You bought two antique lamps for $50 each. Later, you were offered $60 for one and sold it, changed your mind when you saw its duplicate being sold for more, and bought it back for $70. You then sold it for $80. The first one didn't sell at all so you reduced it 10% below what you originally paid and managed to get rid of it. Did you make or lose money on the deal, and how much?

February 18

When Jim was taking a stroll one day, he met his father-in-law's only daughter's mother-in-law. What did he call her?

February 19

A sentence was dropped into the grid below, but the letters dropped out. The letters all appear underneath the squares where they belong, but they have been arranged in their columns alphabetically. A black box in the grid shows a space between words; a dash at the end of a line means that a word continues onto the next line. Can you reassemble the sentence? (Hint: Asking friends to help may be more trouble than it's worth.)

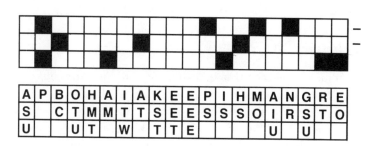

February 20

The following line consists of three countries whose names have been "interlettered." The letters are in the correct order for each country. Unscramble the three countries.

ALUHRUXNGEMEBNOUTRIGNGARAY

February 21

Billy had a coin purse with fifty coins, totaling exactly $1.00. Unfortunately, while counting them, he dropped one coin behind the radiator. What is the probability that it was a penny?

February 22

George Washington was born on February 22, 1732, so we now celebrate President's Day around this date. Each of the following three lines contains three presidents' names. Unscramble them to find the chief executives.

R T O K O E S N E R V N E U L E M D T A N Y
J J T E O F Y F H L E N E R S R O S O N N
T C A O W F O A S T L H I I D N G G E T O N

February 23

(You may have seen this in a slightly different form, but this version has an unusual twist to it.) It was a bring-your-own-food party, but not everybody could contribute food. The agreement was that those who couldn't bring edibles would chip in some cash. Sally brought a certain number of pies, Jane brought one more than Sally, and Hector brought one more than Jane. William brought nothing, but asked them to divide the nice little pies equally, and he would pay. The four split the pies evenly. There was a total of a dozen pies, each worth $1.00. How much should each of them get or pay?

February 24

How many common English words can you make from the letters LGNEA? (There are at least three.) Use all the letters for each word.

February 25

The following silly palindromes—a word, phrase, or sentence reading the same backward as forward as in "Rise to vote, sir"—have the word divisions given. Can you find them?

Debutante is sleeping: ___   ___ ____
Edna and Delia weren't feeling too well:

_ _ _ _ _   _ _ _   _ _ _ _
_ _ _ _ _ .

February 26

Each of the following four words has had the *same* vowel removed. At least three of that vowel are missing from each word. What are the reconstructed words?

PRMAT   RHARS   TNAGR   FORSR

February 27

If 9 is twice 5, how will you write 6 times 5 in the same system of notation? (This type of puzzle dates back to the early Middle Ages, so don't say it isn't logic.)

February 28

What is the highest four-digit number, with no zeros, in which the first digit is one-quarter of the third digit, the second digit is three times the first digit, and the third and last digits are the same?

February 29

Colonel Cholomondely-Snaithwirth-Jones was very proud indeed of his big-game hunting exploits. He had published several monographs about his life among the pygmies, his exploits during the Boer War, and his single-handed capture of an entire tribe of blow-dart hunting natives in Borneo. He had even brought home a poisoned blow dart as evidence, and, as he told friends, he was going to use it to start a collection for the Victoria and Albert Museum. This particular day, dressed in his usual explorer clothes, he was sitting comfortably in an armchair, being interviewed by the Explorers Club membership committee.

"As I said," he continued, "my reputation had spread before me, and these poor chappies sent word via the drums that they needed me desperately. Two of their babies, one of the women, and two warriors had been snatched right out of the village by this man-eating tiger. They were desperately short of warriors, the drums said." He nodded affirmatively. "So I assembled my bearers, my full set of guns, and set off for the village. It was at the headwaters of the Nile, in territory so remote no white man had ever been there. I learned all I could from my bearers about the habits of nocturnal hunters like that tiger—" At this point, each of the four committee members seized one limb of the hapless colonel and threw him down the club's magnificent flight of twenty-two marble steps and onto the street. Why?

March

March was named after Mars, the god of war, by the Romans, who valued military prowess highly. Mars was also the father of Romulus and Remus, the twins who founded Rome.

On March 15, the Ides of March, in 44 B.C., Julius Caesar was assassinated. The senators who stabbed him had grown fearful and jealous of his power; Plutarch reports that some people viewed even his calendar reforms as dictatorial. Incidentally, the Ides usually fell on the thirteenth of the month—only in March, May, July, and October was it the fifteenth. To make that date even less auspicious, United States income tax payments used to be due on the Ides of March. The postponement of tax day to April 15 removed a source of great inspiration for financial writers. *Et tu,* Uncle Sam!

March also brings the vernal equinox for the northern hemisphere, about the twenty-second of the month. The spring and fall equinoxes are the only two dates during the year when day and night are each exactly twelve hours long. The words *spring* and *fall* derive from what leaves do during those seasons: spring from their buds and fall to the ground.

March 1

Which set of numbers would most logically come next in the following sequence?

10 1 9 2 8 3 7 4 6 5 5 6 4 7 3 8 2
(a) 9 1   (b) 9 3   (c) 8 5   (d) 6 7

March 2

The spy was captured easily, and his message proved to be so simple that the lieutenant saw its importance immediately. Here it is. What does it say?

Alice: Tom told Ann Carter Killy and Ted, David Atwood was not moving out now. David awaiting you.

March 3

Rearrange these matchsticks, by touching only *two,* to make a correct equation. (There may be several solutions.)

March 4

The happy couple had decided what to name their expected baby, even though they didn't know whether it would be a boy or a girl. Both their family names contained the letters ODLYL, and names for both sexes could be made from those letters. What were the two names?

March 5

A palindrome is a word or a group of words that reads the same backward and forward. (TENET, for example.) What is the nine-letter palindrome with which the very shy person admitted shyness?

— — — — —   — —   — — .

March 6

Although Jim and Barbara had to buy four presents for various weddings, they found they could not agree on four identical presents. They bought four separate gifts; and the first one cost $5.00 more than the second. The second was half the cost of the first, plus one-third the cost of the first. The third cost two-thirds of the first, and the last cost double the third. They spent a total of $115. What did each of the four cost?

March 7

The names of three foods are mixed up on each of the following lines. The words are given with their letters in correct order, but each word is "interlettered" with the others. Unscramble the foods.

C F H R M E U E E I A S E T T
A P E P P A R L E P L S S U M S

March 8

Using all the letters each time, how many words can you make from the letters REIAMN?

March 9

How many squares of any size are in the diagram below?

March 10

On this date in 1876, Alexander Graham Bell, having spilled acid on himself as motivation, succeeded in sending the first telephone message: "Mr. Watson, come here, I want you." It's a good thing Watson had the only other telephone and Bell didn't have to call Directory Assistance for the number. If three operators can answer 120 calls in half an hour, how many operators does it take to handle 560 calls in one hour?

March 11

Grandma looked up from her rocking chair and said, "As far as I can determine, there is only one anagram of the word TRINKET. What is it?"

March 12

The Puzzleland toy store may go out of business soon because of the owner's idea of pricing. He charges $6 for a doll, $7.50 for a train, $4.50 for a top, and $12 for a paint set. By the same rules, what does he charge for a bicycle?

March 13

People who are afraid of the number 13 are said to have triskaidekaphobia. What are the names for each of the following phobias?

Fear of cats
Fear of foreigners
Fear of open spaces (or of leaving an enclosed space)

March 14

Homonyms are words that sound alike, though they are spelled differently. (Example: to, two, too) One pair of homonyms has meanings that are precisely opposite, and need not be stretched. What are the two spellings of this homonym?

March 15

Which is more, seconds in 100 hours or inches in 100 yards?

March 16

Each of the following words contains the letters MAR. Using the definitions, fill in the blanks:

More insane; colloquially, more angry—also a paint
color: M A _ _ _ R
A shopping area; colloquially, anywhere goods are
sold: MAR _ _ _ _ _ _ _ _
Scanty: M _ A _ _ R

March 17

For Saint Patrick's Day, the letters ERIN have been placed in the box below. Fill in each line so that those four letters are in each row, across, down, and on the long diagonals. No two letters may be the same in any line, nor may two identical letters be next to each other.

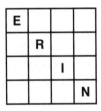

March 18

What relationship to you is your father's only brother's wife's only brother-in-law?

March 19

Each of the following groups of letters can be anagrammed into at least two words. Unscramble the letters.

EFIRSSU   EEMPRSU   EENPRST

March 20

High finance in the kindergarten: Sheree and Tyler's play-store was doing well. Sheree, the more successful shop-keeper, had 75¢ in play money plus 75 percent of what Tyler had. The poor unsuccessful salesman had 50¢ in play money plus half of what Sheree had. How much did each have?

March 21

If three salesmen can sell three stoves in seven minutes, how many stoves can six salesmen sell in seventy minutes?

March 22

> This is an Izaak Walton tale.
> As the fish hung by its tail,
> The angler proudly had it weighed.
> "Three-fourths of its total," he then said,
> "Plus three-fourths of three-fourths of a pound
> Will give the whole, exact, not round."

March 23

How many words can you make from the letters *CEEIPR,* using all the letters each time?

March 24

You can substitute one letter for the first letter of each word in the following pairs and make two new words (Example: RACE ___P___ CLAY = PACE—PLAY). Then insert the new letter on the line between the words, and you will spell a new word reading down.

TALL	____	LABEL
SOUND	____	COUGH
SLIT	____	HIM
ALL	____	ARE
ROSE	____	TETHER

March 25

You would really like to stay longer at the party, because you are having such a good time. Unfortunately, it's getting very late. You realize that if it were one hour later, it would be twice as long past midnight as it would be if it were only right now. When you start thinking like that, you've been up too long. What time is it now?

March 26

Each of the following words includes the letters MAR. Using the definitions, fill in the words.

An unusual type of boat:
$$\_ \ \_ \ \_ \ \_ \ M \ A \ R \ \_ \ \_$$
An Italian seafood: $\_ \ \_ \ \_ \ \_ \ M \ A \ R \ \_$

A title of nobility:
$$M \ A \ R \ \_ \ \_ \ \_ \ \_ \ \_ \ \_ \ \_$$

March 27

Only one word can be anagrammed from SPRINGIEST. What is it?

March 28

March usually brings warmer weather. Can you go from COLD to WARM on paper in only four steps? Change one letter each time, forming a new word each time.

C	O	L	D
—	—	—	—
—	—	—	—
—	—	—	—
W	A	R	M

March 29

The following diagram has eight sections. Each of them contains four letters, with a question mark in the middle showing that one letter is missing. Your job is to find the one letter that is missing and then rearrange the letters in each section to form eight words. You may find the same letters in two sets of boxes. This merely means that two words can be made from the same letters. Find them both, in that case.

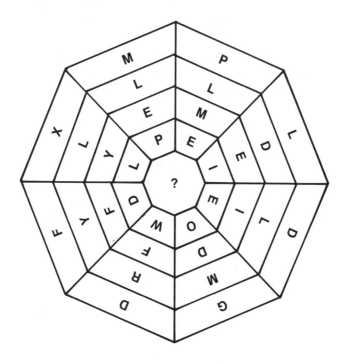

March 30

Your brother is color blind and, since he has four different colors of socks in his drawer, he usually just pulls out the first two and wears a mismatched pair. He has blue, brown, black, and blue-and-white-striped socks in the drawer in the ratio of 8 blue to 6 brown, to 6 black, to 8 blue-and-white. How many socks would he have to pull out before he could be certain of having a matched pair?

March 31

Tony likes indigo but not blue. He likes onions but not turnips; he likes forms but not shapes. According to the same rule does he like tomatoes or avocados?

April

There is some evidence that the Romans named their month *Aphrilis* after Aphrodite, the Greek goddess of love. Aphrodite metamorphosed into the Roman goddess Venus, just as Zeus became Jupiter, Ares became Mars, and other foreign deities adapted to the new culture. The Romans considered the month of April sacred to Venus. In the *Odyssey,* Homer tells how Ares and Aphrodite fell in love with each other, so perhaps it is fitting that they are so close together in the calendar.

April 1 has been the day for "fooling" since sometime in the seventeenth century. The French say *poisson d'Avril,* "April fish," for the poor soul who is the victim of such a joke. One favorite stunt used to be to phone somebody who was out of the office, leave a message to call Mr. Fox, and give the number of the zoo. The Bronx Zoo, and many others, have stopped taking calls for Mr. Fox on April 1.

April 1

Here's one to try on April Fools. What would you call your ex-spouse's former daughter-in-law's first husband's daughter?

April 2

The same five letters, rearranged to make two different words, can fill in the blanks below. Complete the sentences.

"I had to fire that nincompoop," said the boss. "Our company _ _ _ _ _ somebody a lot less _ _ _ _ _ ."

April 3

The names of three mammals are hidden in the following sentences. Find them. All the letters are in the correct order.

The large crowd at the flea market came looking for bargains.
I took off the peel and ate the banana.
He has no judgment, no sense altogether.

April 4

If TEN = 20 − 5 − 14; and MEN = 13 − 5 − 14; what do WOMEN equal by the same logic?

April 5

You are working out some estimates for your boss. You can come up with a very good package for your nice little widgets, but the packaging may be too expensive. The cost of the widget and the packaging is $1.10, and the widget is $1.00 more than the package. How much will you have to tell your boss that the package for each widget will cost?

April 6

You've been standing at a bus stop in the April rain. The transportation system in your town is not very effective. You waited fifteen minutes and then a group of buses came along together. The first was too crowded, so you took the last. There was one bus ahead of another bus, one bus behind another bus, one bus behind two buses, and one bus with two ahead of it. What is the smallest number of buses there could have been in that bunch?

April 7

You are decorating for spring, and you've found a bargain: a huge box of beautiful decorated tiles, enough to provide a border in two rooms. You really can't figure out how to arrange them, however. If you set a border of two tiles all around, there's one left over; if you set three tiles all around, or four, or five, or six, there's still one tile left over. Finally, you try a block of seven tiles for each corner, and you come out even. What is the smallest number of tiles you could have to get this result?

April 8

One four-letter word will fit on all three lines below to make new words with the word preceding and the word following. (Example: IN _(DOOR)_ STOP) The same 4-letter word must be used for all 3 lines. What's the word?

BACK	____	SOME
FREE	____	MADE
SECOND	____	BAG

April 9

If today is Monday, what is the day after the day before the day before tomorrow?

April 10

Mensaman flew to Puzzleland at the fantastic speed of 1000 miles per hour. There he picked up his ever faithful friend and flew back, burdened by the extra weight, at only 500 miles per hour. What was his average speed?

April 11

In this type of verse, "first" and "second" and so on refer to the individual letters of a word. Find the correct letter for each definition or explanation, and complete the word.

> My first is in sugar but not in tea
> My second in swim but not in sea
> My third in apple and also pear
> My fourth in ring and also hare
> My last in ten but not in herd
> My whole a very complimentary word.

April 12

The following multiplication example uses every digit from 0 to 9 once (not counting the intermediate steps). Fill in the missing numbers.

$$
\begin{array}{r}
7\ x\ x \\
4\ x \\
\hline
x\ x\ x\ x\ x
\end{array}
$$

April 13

The same five letters can be anagrammed into four different words to fill in the blanks in the sentence to make (somewhat) good sense. What are missing words?

The farmer with hundreds of __ __ __ __ __ , deeply __ __ __ __ __ about the amount of rainfall, and __ __ __ __ __ around with artificial watering systems when the ground is dry enough to __ __ __ __ __ him about the possibility of crop failure.

April 14

Which set of numbers would most logically fill in the blanks in the following series?

101 99 102 98 103 97 __ __ 105 95 104 94
(a) 101 98   (b) 104 96   (c) 106 99
              (d) none of these

April 15

An aphorism is indicated below. All the vowels have been removed and the remaining letters broken into groups of four letters each. Replace the vowels to read the saying.

NFFC   NTBS   NSSW   MNWH   FNDM
CHNT   HTWL   DDHL   FHRW   RKBG
HTTW.

April 16

It was time to send the kids to camp, and Sally and Jim were shopping for supplies. They spent half the money they had plus $4.00 on socks for the kids; half of what was then left plus $3.00 on name tapes; and half of what was then left plus $2.00 on a small wallet for each child. They found themselves with $3.00 left over, so they treated themselves to a glass of iced tea each. How much did they start with? (Hint—work backward.)

April 17

What is the five-digit number, no zeroes, in which the second digit is three times the first, the third is one more than the second, the fourth is four times the first, and the last is one-half more than the second?

April 18

When the two met, one was half the other's age plus seven years. Ten years later, when they married, the bride was thirty, but this time one was nine-tenths the age of the other. How old was the groom? (No fractions, no partial years—whole numbers only)

April 19

The engineering department was arranging for a rather expensive catered lunch to bid farewell to their retiring colleague. They calculated that it would cost each person $30. One good mathematician remarked, "It's lucky that there aren't five fewer of us to split the bill, or it would be $10 more from each." How many engineers split the bill, and how much did it cost?

April 20

There are many English words to which you can add one *s* to make plural nouns. There are very few that become singular again if you add another *s*. Can you name two?

April 21

Complete the last square of letters, using the same system as followed in the previous four squares.

T H	U Z	I S	E O	U A
P	E	D	Q	?
S I	L Z	A M	S F	E R

April 22

If Boston is east of New York, cross out all the A's. If not, cross out the R's. If Paris is south of New York, cross out all the O's. If not, cross out the I's. If Sri Lanka is in Asia, cross out the B's and U's. If not, cross out the C's. The remaining letters will tell you whether you've found the right answer.

C A A O I I A B U R R I A U E I B B C I A U T

April 23

The Order of the Garter, a prestigious award for English knights, was founded this day in 1349. (It's the day of Saint George, patron saint of England and fabled dragon slayer.) See if you deserve an award by unscrambling the following thirteen letters into a common English word.

A T C S D R I E I N O N O

April 24

Mother was very proud of her lace tablecloth, which was an heirloom. She was most upset when the children came home from school and put their dirty school books on it. She said (start at the correct letter, and move in any direction to a touching letter):

```
T  I  P  S  S
L  O  O  O  K
T  H  O  O  B
E  L  T  M  Y
C  O  H  A  N
```

April 25

You can replace the letters below with numbers, so that the addition will be correct numerically. (Hint: K = 9)

```
    M O M
    M O M
      N O
  ---------
  B O O K
```

April 26

The logic professor posted a notice on his class door: "Class is canceled today on account of spring. We will meet again at 1:00 P.M. three days after two days before the day before tomorrow." What day does the class meet?

April 27

Dot likes pots and pans but not cooks. She likes straw but not hay; she likes sagas but not poems. Does she like a star or a planet?

April 28

The lovely but not-terribly-bright contessa was swindled of her jewels. She knew that her beautiful diamond pin had nine diamonds down each side, and nine across the top and bottom, clustered as shown below, but she had never really examined the arrangement closely. A clever thief had figured out a way to steal four of the magnificent diamonds so that the contessa never missed them. He had reset the diamonds so that there were still nine diamonds on each side of the pin, but only twenty diamonds in all. How did he reset the jewels to get away with four of them?

```
┌─────────┐
│ 3  3  3 │
│ 3     3 │
│ 3  3  3 │
└─────────┘
```

April 29

Each of the following words contains the letters APR somewhere. Using the definitions, fill in the words.

A fruit:	A P R __ __ __ __
Took by force:	__ A P __ __ R __ __
Sign of the zodiac:	__ A P R __ __ __ __ __

April 30

It's hard to keep within a budget, Maura discovered as she prepared her class's May Day party. She had been assigned money from the common fund, and she spent half of it plus $2.00 for a nice cake. Then she spent half of what she had left plus $2.00 for baskets and flowers. Then she spent half of what she had left plus $1.00 for candy. At that point she was out of money. How much had she started with?

May

There are two different theories about how May got its name. Some experts say it was named for the goddess Maia, the mother of Hermes. Others say that Caesar named the month to honor the *Major,* the senior branch of the Roman Senate, and that he named June not for Juno, but for the *Junior* branch of the Senate. You can take your pick—there isn't anyone around today who remembers just why those names were chosen.

May Day, before it acquired its present connotation as a worker's holiday, had far more rural roots. For centuries it was a British, and then American, custom to gather flowers on the first of May and hang baskets of freshly picked blooms on the doorknobs of friends' houses. Louisa May Alcott mentions this custom several times in her books. Dancing around the Maypole is another time-honored ritual. For anyone who didn't go through teacher-training classes forty or more years ago, this is the procedure. A tall pole is set up with long ribbons of different colors attached to the top. Each ribbon is taken by a separate dancer, who weaves in and out among the other dancers around the pole. Eventually the pole is wrapped in many colors, and the dancers are left standing right at the pole with a few inches of ribbon in their hands. It isn't as easy as it sounds!

May 1

To start the month right, figure out the word concealed in the following poem. (First, second, etc., refer to letters of a word.) By selecting the right letter you will come up with an appropriate word.

> My first is in silly but not in fool
> My second in pupil but not in school
> My third in read and also write
> My fourth in glimpse and also light
> My fifth in ten but not in three
> My last in glad and also glee
> My whole a season of the year
> That's clue enough to solve it here.

May 2

Why are 1980 pennies worth more than 1979 pennies?

May 3

The following three lines contain the names of U.S. cities, one city per line. Find the hidden cities.

> We were no longer interested in returning there because of the bad weather.
> "I am sorry to tell you that you have injured your lumbar region," said the doctor.
> I would be happy to join you, but temporary problems keep me away.

May 4

If SIX is TEN, ONE is HIS, and FIVE is LEGS, what is SEVEN?

May 5

What is the word coiled inside this circle?

```
      T  P
  I         U
  A         N
      L  S
```

May 6

The same five letters can be rearranged into two separate words to fill in the blanks.

The caveman shook a primitive sort of _ _ _ _ _ . It was too heavy to use against some of the faster animals, but it seemed to work against _ _ _ _ _ .

May 7

You have one of those fancy double boilers whose lid fits either pot. They aren't very heavy pots, either. The bigger pot weighs 12 ounces by itself; with the lid on, it weighs twice as much as the little pot without the cover. The little pot, with the lid on, weighs one-third more than the big pot all by itself. What does the pot lid weigh by itself?

May 8

Each of the following words contains the letters MAY. Using the definitions, fill in the missing letters and complete the word.

A creamy dressing made with eggs and oil:

M A Y _ _ _ _ _ _ _

Astonishingly: _ M A _ _ _ _ _ Y

May 9

Back at the Puzzleland toy store, the proprietor has priced a game at 14¢, a doll at 21¢, a koala bear at 28¢, and a top at 14¢. Using the same logic (or lack of it), how much does he charge for a pinwheel?

May 10

Andy likes orange but not purple. He likes torches but not chandeliers. He eats berries but not fruits. Following the same rules, does he like Byron or Keats?

May 11

Ages seem to be perennially fascinating to puzzle writers, so why fight it? Of three sisters named April, May, and June, none is yet twenty-one. April is now as old as June was fourteen years ago, and two-thirds of May's age. May, on the other hand, will be June's age when May is twice as old as she is now plus two years. Three years ago, May was as old as April is now. How old are April, May, and June?

May 12

The first word of the following word square (the words read the same down and across) has been filled in for you. Fill in the remaining words so that you use three E's; two each S, L, O, G, R, and A; and one T in total for the whole square.

```
O  G  R  E
G
R
E
```

May 13

Take the number of states before Alaska and Hawaii were added. Double that and add the number of "winds." Then subtract the number of Ali Baba's thieves, not counting Ali Baba. Divide by the number of days in May minus 1. Cube the result. What do you get?

May 14

You have fifty coins totaling $1.00. You drop one down an open drain while tossing the coins in your hand. What is the chance that you have lost a quarter?

May 15

A "Tom Swifty" is a pun based on Tom's extraordinary expressiveness: "Hand me the eggbeater," said Tom stirringly. A "Tom Swifty" punning sentence is encoded below. All the vowels, including Y, have been removed, and the letters broken into groups of three. Reconstitute the sentence.

THR   SNW   TRS   DTM   DRL.

May 16

Four of the words below have one significant feature in common which distinguishes them from the fifth word. Which is the odd man out?

REACT   TRACE   CARTE
CATER   SCARE

May 17

A definition was dropped into the boxes below. Each of the letters shown is in its proper column, but they have been arranged alphabetically. The black boxes show the spaces between words; a dash at the end of a line shows where a word has been broken. Fill in the definition.

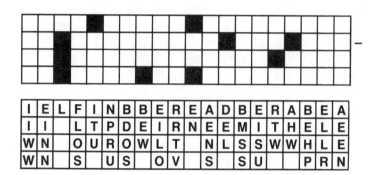

I	E	L	F	I	N	B	B	E	R	E	A	D	B	E	R	A	B	E	A
I	I		L	T	P	D	E	I	R	N	E	E	M	I	T	H	E	L	E
W	N		O	U	R	O	W	L	T		N	L	S	S	W	W	H	L	E
W	N		S		U	S		O	V		S		S	U			P	R	N

May 18

The alleged perpetrator was trying to get even with his foe. This all happened in Puzzleland, so it was easy for him to obtain a sack of magic gunpowder to carry off to his enemy's fort. He did not realize, however, that the powder was self-igniting, and it had been leaking since he stole it. He had been running at his usual magic speed of 14 miles per hour over the 28-mile distance, but had to hide for a while when he reached his enemy's fort. Meanwhile, that magic gunpowder was burning itself up along his trail at the rate of 12 miles per hour. How long could he hide without making a spectacle of himself?

May 19

Somehow or other I got talked into buying something on the installment plan. I'm not sure I got a good deal. The payments to date, according to my checkbook, have reached $96. The second year cost $2.00 more than the first year; the third year cost $3.00 more than the second; and the fourth year cost me $4.00 more than the third. What were my payments the first year?

May 20

The following coiled sentence, when you find the proper starting letter and move in any direction to a touching letter, will finish the quatrain below. There is one null letter. Each letter is used once only. (Hint: A common problem in labs)

> The head of the research lab said one day,
> Looking solemn and sad and grave,

```
T  E  A  T  R  O  E  E  X
O  H  D  A  P  V  M  V  A
N  L  Y  T  O  E  R  S  T
E  R  A  T  H  G  I  O  N
T  H  O  S  E  I  D  I  D
```

May 21

One letter, a different one for each line, has been removed from each of the words below. The missing letters appear at least three times (and sometimes more) in each word. Fill in the missing letter for each word and reconstruct the words. The letters are also scrambled, just to make it a little harder.

FILPRT   PSVRR

May 22

The following cryptogram has been done in a simple substitution cipher: each number represents a letter, and the same number always represents the same letter. What does it say?

14 26 23 26 14 22   24 6 9 18 22
24 26 15 15 22 23.   8 26 18 23   8 19 22
4 26 8   20 22 7 7 18 13 20
20 15 12 4 18 13 20   9 22 11 12 9 7 8
12 13   19 22 9   4 12 9 16.

May 23

In this addition alphametic, you can replace each letter with a number (the same number for each letter), to find a correct arithmetical solution. (Hint: A = 1)

```
        H A N G
        H A N G
        H A N G
       ---------
        G A N G S
```

May 24

In the puzzle below, change the first letter of each word on either side of the blank to make a new word. Use the same letter for both words on one line. Then fill in the new letter on the line between the two words. When you have finished, you will have a new word, reading down.

MART	_____	HARD
ROUND	_____	WERE
FASTER	_____	WITHER
PLASTIC	_____	FAST
BOLES	_____	AIMLESS

May 25

Six seamstresses could sew six seams in twenty minutes. How many seamstresses would be needed to sew thirty-six seams in two hours?

May 26

The following circle contains all the letters except one of six words, one in each pie-shaped section. The letters have been scrambled. When you unscramble them, you will find that the missing letter, which will complete each word properly, is quite clear. Find the missing letter and the words.

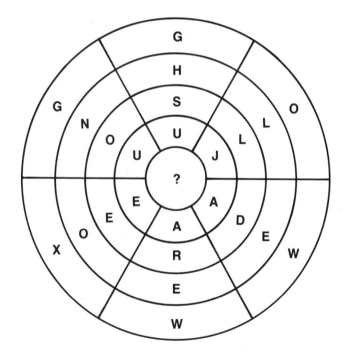

May 27

You've bought your weekly egg supply at the local farm store. The first morning you have company for breakfast and use half the eggs plus one-half an egg. The next morning you use one-half of what's left plus one-half an egg. The third morning you use one-half of what's left plus one-half an egg, and on the fourth morning, you're down to one solitary egg, so you make French toast. In all this cooking, you've never had one-half an egg to carry over to the next day. How many eggs did you buy originally?

May 28

You are female. What relationship to you is your father's only son-in-law's mother-in-law's only daughter?

May 29

Which set of letters would logically come next in the following sequence?

A Y D V G S J P M M P J ? ?
(a) R K (b) S G (c) R S (d) S I

May 30

My quiz for this day, May 30, is most unusual. As is this paragraph. What is so unusual about it? If you look hard, you should find what it is without too much difficulty. Try hard to spot it. How long did you think about it?

May 31

As you may recall, a palindrome is a word or group of words that reads the same backward as forward (Madam I'm Adam). Definitions for two palindromes are given below, as well as the number of letters. Complete the palindromes.

Unselfish mother, says caring child.

— —   — —   — —
— — — — — — — —   — —   —
— — .

A scarlet alcoholic beverage is homicide, politely.

— — —   — — —   — — —   — —
— — — — — —

June

June is now a popular month for weddings, but it was not always so. September used to be the favored month and, in farm communities, marrying after the harvest was still more popular. But way back, the Romans considered June the luckiest month for marriages, and May the unluckiest.

One interesting June custom dates from the Middle Ages, when, in the English village of Dunmow, a flitch of bacon was awarded to any husband and wife who could swear that they would marry each other again, had not quarreled for a year, and had never regretted their marriage. There are only a few records of couples bringing home the bacon. Married life was probably similar to its current state, and village life provided little privacy, hence not much opportunity for false swearing.

Around the twenty-first of June comes the summer solstice—the date on which the sun reaches the most northerly point in the zodiac. It is also the longest day of the year, and the beginning of summer—at least for the northern hemisphere. The earth is farther from the sun in June than it is in December, but the sun's rays strike the northern hemisphere more directly, and thus provide more heat.

June 1

There seems to be only one other word that can be made from the letters in the word IMPORTUNATE. Find it.

June 2

All its vowels have been removed from the following rather cynical statement, and the remaining letters have been broken into groups of three letters each. Reconstruct the sentence.

PDS   TRN   SCM   NTW   SRT   STH
QCK   NDT   HDD

June 3

The following cryptogram is simple substitution of an unusual sort. Each letter or symbol represents one letter, the same one each time. Decipher the sentence.

JS$\frac{11}{44}$OMRDD   OD   S   DYPVL   YJSY
D$\frac{1}{4}$;OYD   YJTRR   GPT   PMR   YJR
FSU   SGYRT   UPI   NIU   OY.

June 4

By using all the digits 1 through 9, it is possible to construct four addition examples with the sum 873. Reversing the top and bottom numbers is not permitted. Each combination must be different. One number in each set has been filled in to give you a head start.

x x 4	x x 9	x 5 x	x x x
x x x	x x x	x x x	6 x x
8 7 3	8 7 3	8 7 3	8 7 3

June 5

One of the most famous puzzles in the math world is "How Old Is Ann?" Here's another variation. Ann is now exactly two-fifths of her older sister's age, and two years from now she will be one-half of her older sister's age. Conversely, two years ago, Ann was only one-fourth the age of her older sister's age at that time. How old is Ann now? (She's a fairly young child, by the way.)

June 6

You have stealthily raided your small child's piggy bank. You feel slightly guilty as you count the money. You have the same number of dimes and quarters, totaling exactly $2.45. When you turn honest and put it back, how many of each coin will you need to replace? (Your child keeps a record of how much she puts in and in what denomination, of course.)

June 7

When Maria went to get a passport, she had to give her real date of birth, but under all other circumstances she refused. When somebody asked how old she was, she said she was twenty-one, mentally omitting all Sundays. Sundays she didn't work, so naturally she didn't get any older. How old was Maria really?

June 8

What would logically come next in this sequence?

S30   031   N30

June 9

The following sentence has two blanks. The same six letters, rearranged, can be used to make two different words which will fill the blanks appropriately. Find the words.

The little woodland _ _ _ _ _ _ was having a wonderful time playing with all the animals in the woods; unfortunately, she had no previous knowledge of the pretty furry little animal with the peculiar _ _ _ _ _ _ , but soon was sadder and wiser.

June 10

Barbara is a young lady with decided tastes. She likes khaki but not brown; she likes rendezvous but not meetings; she likes mousses but not jellies. Does she like jodhpurs or riding pants?

June 11

This slightly jumbled version of a nursery rhyme has had all its vowels removed and the words have been broken up (or down) into groups of three letters each. Replace the vowels to decipher the sentence.

JCK   BNM   BLJ   CKB   QCK   FRT
HLG   HTJ   STC   HNG   DND   THR
DSS   LCK.

June 12

Which would you rather have, half a dozen dozen dimes or a dozen and a half dimes?

June 13

Two of the four boxes *cannot* be made from the unfolded cube shown below. Which ones are they?

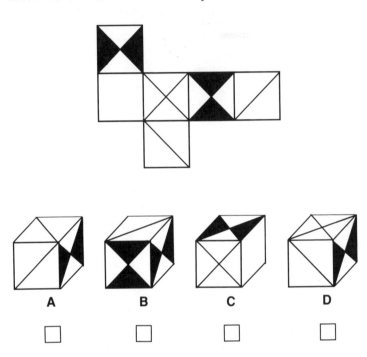

A	B	C	D
☐	☐	☐	☐

June 14

If you reverse the digits of my age, you have the age of my son. A year ago, I was twice his age. How old are we both now?

June 15

You're so desperate to find a job that you're even looking in Liar and Truthteller Town. That's a special part of Puzzleland where half the people always tell the truth, half the people always lie, and outsiders have no way to tell them apart by sight.

You're waiting in the reception room for your interview, feeling nervous. An attractive young lady next to you whispers she is sure that the previous applicant won't get the job because she heard him admit that he was a Liar, and obviously unemployable. Then the interviewer calls you in.

"I'm wearing a blue suit," he says, and indeed he is, so you know that he's a Truthteller. "I need to test your logical reasoning for the position we now have open. What can you tell me about the young lady who talked to you outside?"

The job depends on your answer. What have you decided about the woman in the reception room?

June 16

It's not easy having a mathematics professor as a new friend. When she invites you to her house she says, "All the houses on my side of the street are numbered consecutively in even numbers. There are six houses on my side of my block and the sum of their numbers is 9870. You don't know which block I live on, and it's a long, long street, but I will tell you that I live in the lowest number on my side of the block. What's the number? Or are you just going to ring the first even-numbered doorbell for twenty blocks?

June 17

The following brief message has been broken into letters.
Each letter has been placed below its proper position in the
diagram, but the letters have been put in alphabetical order.
The black spaces show word divisions. Fill in the saying.

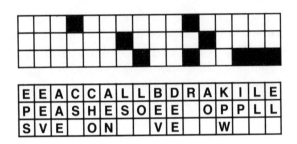

June 18

In Puzzleland's silly grocery store down the block, the proprietor has decided to price his produce a certain way. A daf-
fodil (he sells flowers too) is worth 10¢; a carrot is worth 8¢;
a peach is worth 5¢; a zucchini is worth 10¢. What is a plum
worth?

June 19

You have ten coins totaling 49¢. By an odd coincidence, so
does your friend Henry with whom you are walking. One of
you accidentally loses a coin through a hole in a pocket.
What is the chance it is a dime?

June 20

While Isabelle was out walking one day with her husband, Ferdinand, she met Cristoforo, who was her only sister's mother-in-law's only son's grandfather-in-law. What was his relationship to Ferdinand and Isabelle?

June 21

Each of the following jumbled words has had at least three of the same letter removed from it, a different letter from each word. Find the missing letters to reconstruct the words.

YTHLNM   AEEHNRU   DEINNOI

June 22

You've finally decided to clean under the chair and sofa cushions. To your great pleasure you find you have $1.80 in all, the same number of nickels and quarters. How many of each have you found?

June 23

All the following words contain the letters JUN somewhere. (Those letters may in fact appear more than once.) Using the definitions, fill in the words.

A lower professorial rank; also an addition to:

__ __ J U N __ __

A person not legally an adult:

J U __ __ N __ __ __

A kind of berry or shrub: J U N __ __ __ __

A diary, a record of daily events:

J __ U __ N __ __

June 24

After escaping from the earthquake, flood, and tornado which had afflicted his city, all the poor shopkeeper could dig out of the rubble of his store was four pairs of weights and a balance scale. Fortunately, he was good at math, and found that he could weigh anything from one pound to 170 pounds with the four pairs (please note: pairs, not individual weights). What were the four pairs of weights?

June 25

How many common English words can you make from the letters EHISTTW? All letters must be used each time.

June 26

The names of three countries appear in the paragraph below. All the letters of each country are in the proper order. Can you discover the names?

> Interpol and the FBI were working on the same case. "How can a daily routine be so varied?" asked the chief. "Oh, just watch the lady decked in diamonds," Agent Hobart replied. "She changes her route every day."

June 27

Darlene likes 225 but not 224; she likes 900 but not 800; she likes 144 but not 145. Does she like 1600 or 1700?

June 28

You just dumped a bag of fruit into the deepest end of the fruit bin, and now you can't see what you have. They're all smooth skinned, and about the same size, so you can't tell by touch either. You know you have five large plums, five nectarines, and five small smooth-skinned peaches. How many pieces of fruit must you take out to be absolutely sure of getting a plum?

June 29

So far as we can determine, only one other word can be made from the letters of INSATIABLE. Find it.

June 30

Each of the following three sets of letters has been made up of items relating to June weddings. Unscramble the three items in each set. All the letters are in their proper order.

B B O R U V I Q D U E E E S T M A I I D L

G R H I O R N N E O G Y O M O M O N

M F L O W E T D H O E W R E D I I N N R G
L G M A A I W R R C L H

July

July had a bad reputation in classical times. Because of the heat, and the illnesses the heat caused, the Romans felt it was under the influence of the unfriendly star Canicula, the "Little Dog." They called the days from July 3 to August 11, which then corresponded to the rising and setting of this star, the "Dog Days."

Three western countries celebrate their national holidays in July: Canada on the first, the United States on the fourth, and France on the fourteenth. Perhaps the July heat makes people dissatisfied enough with their governments to revolt. More likely it just makes them want a holiday. Canada became independent peacefully in 1867. The American Revolution had been going on for over a year when the Declaration of Independence was signed on July 4, 1776. And the storming of the Bastille in Paris on July 14, 1789, was just the start of a series of revolutions in France. Since then, France has had five republics, four kings, and two emperors.

July 1

Tom is younger than Rose, but older than Will and Jack, in that order. Rose is younger than Susie, but older than Jack.

Jack is younger than Jim. Susie is older than Rose, but younger than Jim. Jim is older than Tom. Who is the oldest?

July 2

Jemima has the same number of brothers as she has sisters, but her brother Roland has twice as many sisters as he has brothers. How many boys and girls are there in the family?

July 3

The following multiplication example uses all the digits from 0 to 9 once and once only (not counting the intermediate steps). Finish the problem. One number has been filled in to get you started.

$$
\begin{array}{r}
\text{x x x} \\
\text{x 5} \\
\hline
\text{x x x x x}
\end{array}
$$

July 4

If King George IV was ruler of England during the American Revolution, cross out all the N's, I's, and D's. If not, cross out all the O's, U's, and B's. If Paul Revere was not a real person, cross out all the E's and P's. If he was real, cross out the W's, R's, and S's. If General Lafayette fought on the side of the Colonies, cross out the X's, F's, and T's. If not, cross out all the C's. Well?

I B O N U U D W E R P S E S N S D X E X N F C T E T

July 5

You leave your job interview in Liar and Truthteller Town with two other candidates, who seem to know each other. The interviewer has told you that one of them is a Liar and one is a Truthteller, but you were so nervous you didn't ask him which was which.

Out on the sidewalk the three of you find the local Witch selling apples from a booth. Wicked witches are notorious for making apples that will put you to sleep for one hundred years, and you have a train to catch. But those apples look delicious. So you turn to the other candidates and randomly ask one for advice. Her answer tells you all you need to know about the local Witch's apples. What was your question?

July 6

The coiled sentence below contains the lines that will complete the following rhyme. By starting at the correct spot and moving letter by letter in any direction—up, down, sideways, and diagonally—you can work it out. (The square contains two null letters that don't appear in the lines.)

> As Hans was walking up the Alps,
> A vision turned his head.
> With Mother on his handlebars
> Along the road Fritz sped.
> They hit a curve!

```
H  E  O  K  E  J  U
S  P  O  L  E  T  S
A  H  K  O  C  N  O
N  S  N  O  M  A  H
B  B  D  I  A  S  E
```

July 7

There is a very odd zoo on the planet XzyQE. It houses animals with two heads and three legs and animals with two heads and two legs. A count reveals that there are 102 heads and 134 legs in all. How many of each kind of animal are there?

July 8

The brilliant but not entirely sensible inventor had discovered three separate ways to save fuel while driving. Each one saved approximately 30 percent on fuel consumption. "Aha," said the brilliant inventor, "I will use only 10 percent of the fuel I now use and save a great deal of money." Unfortunately, it didn't work out that way. How much fuel did he save, assuming that all the savings were independent and cumulative?

July 9

Jack and Jill were racing, but it was no contest. Jack beat Jill by 10 yards on a 100-yard course. Jill suggested that for the second race, Jack should start 10 yards behind the starting line—she figured that would give her a fair chance, since he had won by 10 yards. Who won, and by how much?

July 10

The young fellow was extremely eager to join his girlfriend for dinner. It was a 24-mile run upstream to visit her. His boat's speed would be 14 miles per hour but the current is running 4 miles an hour against him. He just filled his tank and he knows he has 20 gallons, but he uses up 6 gallons per hour. Will he make it or will he run out of gas?

July 11

Each of the following four words is the name of a bird, but most of the letters have been removed. Fill in the blanks to get the names of the birds.

L _ _ W I _ _
P _ _ _ E _
_ R _ B _
_ A _ _ I _ A _

July 12

As an antiques dealer located, of course, in Puzzleland, you are used to taking a loss now and then. The genuine Louis XIV TV set you bought has proved very difficult to sell. You priced it originally at $100. Then you marked it down to $80. Then you marked it down to $64. Following your same rules, how much will its price be after the next markdown? (You realize, of course, that Louis XIV TV sets are hard to sell; they aren't state of the art.)

July 13

Another Tom Swifty. Follow the rules and trace from letter to letter in any direction. One null letter to fill in a space.

```
I  L  I  P  S
K  T  Y  L  I
E  H  X  R  C
E  S  S  A  M
E  C  S  I  O
H  I  P  D  T
```

July 14

Today is Bastille Day, the French national holiday, so this question is in honor of the French people's love of good food.

Pierre stopped at his favorite wine shop to buy a bottle of Sauternes for the celebration. He spent half of what he had plus $2.00 for a very special bottle of Château d'Yquem. Then he spent half of what he had left plus $3.00 for a small tin of foie gras. Then he stopped at his favorite bakery and bought brioches to spread the foie gras on, and spent half of what he had left, plus $4.00. At that point, he had $2.00 left, with which he bought a small bottle of digestive medicine, just in case. How much did he have to begin with?

July 15

The same four-letter word can be added to each of the following words to make a new word or a common phrase. What is the word?

BOUND   PROOF   TREE   LESS   BIRD

July 16

The Great Detective is hot on the trail of the guilty party who has perpetrated some atrocious puns. "Intent to deceive" is the charge, and he is now interrogating three suspects. George says, "I'm innocent—Jane is too." Jane says, "Sally did it, and George is innocent." Sally says, "I'm innocent and Jane did it." The guilty one lied, and the innocent both told the truth. Who is the perpetrator?

July 17

A particular plan has been followed to determine the middle
number in each diagram. Fill in the missing number.

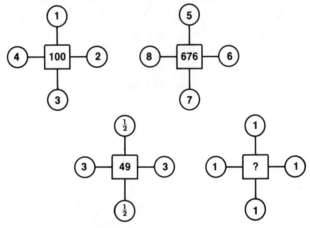

July 18

Simon Walton was an inveterate fisherman, and his wife an
inveterate objector—especially to cleaning fish. This time,
he cut off her objections before they started by announcing
that he had sold his fish to another fisherman. "And it was
a fairly large one, too," he said. "The fish weighed ten pounds
plus half its own weight." How many pounds of fish had he
sold?

July 19

Your solar clock isn't working perfectly. Each day, in broad
sunlight, it picks up half a minute, and each night, in the
darkness, it loses one-third of a minute. In how many days,
starting at sunrise on the first day, will it be five minutes
fast? (Assuming that daylight and darkness are constant, of
course, or the puzzle won't work.)

July 20

Each of the following words contains the letters JUL. The letters may appear in the word more than once but are only shown once. Using the definitions given, fill in the words.

One of Shakespeare's heroines: J U L __ __ __
A flower: J __ __ __ U __ L
Extremely happy, shouting for joy:
                          J U __ __ L __ __ __

July 21

Palindromes read the same forward and backward (Otto or Madam, I'm Adam), and can be words or phrases or whole sentences. Here are some definitions.

What you do when the walls of your apartment are
    no longer fresh: __ __ __ __ __ __ __
First appearance on television:

        __ __ __ __   __ __ __ __ __

July 22

How many triangles are in this drawing?

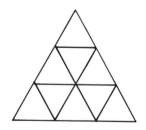

July 23

There was a fabric sale going on at Caveat Emptor Yard Goods. True to his store's name, the owner had a slightly short yardstick—3 inches short, to be exact, which he wasn't. However, to make up for this, and so he wouldn't lose too many customers, he added 5 percent to whatever yard goods he gave, which was usually enough. This time, however, Sally ordered 5 yards of curtain material, having measured her windows very, very exactly. Was she short or over? (When you figure, remember that he gave the additional 5 percent on his short yard measure, not on a regular yard!)

July 24

I personally don't care for health fiends. I refuse to do what is good for me. I stroll daily at 2 miles per hour. One of my jogger friends said, "Why don't you jog? You'd cover the same distance—12 miles—and save a lot of time." I found out that he jogs exactly three times as fast as I stroll. How much time would I save if I jogged alongside him?

July 25

The same seven letters, rearranged into two different words, can be used to fill in the blanks below. Fill in the blanks to complete the sentences.

"What happened to your constant
_ _ _ _ _ _ _ ?" asked the lady with
the parasol, having the driver stop her carriage
to ask this most indiscreet question. "Well," said
the lady in the bustle gown who had just returned
to town for a visit, "Didn't you hear? We
_ _ _ _ _ _ _ ."

July 26

If you have a good memory and a big vocabulary, you may be able to come up with at least three words containing all five vowels, A, E, I, O, and U. The vowels don't have to appear in order (though they can be), and you don't have to include Y (though you can).

July 27

The local recycling plant had a contract requiring anyone who obtained recycled bottles for storage from them, to bring them back to be recycled again. The plant could make one new bottle from every seven bottles returned. One week, on Monday, they got 343 bottles to recycle. Assuming that everybody brought back all the empties, how many could they eventually remake from the 343?

July 28

The following word square is a little more complicated than the previous ones. It has five letters, not four, across and down. Fill it in so that it contains, in addition to the letters shown, one each, R and I; two each, T, O, and L; three E's; and five S's.

```
H A B I T
A
B
I
T
```

July 29

Your boss has gone out of town. Her secretary is angry at you for some reason, so he tells you, "She wants to see you in her office at 8:30 A.M. two days after the day before the day after tomorrow." What day will you show up half an hour early to see your boss? Today is Tuesday.

July 30

You can buy four chocolate bars and three peanut butter cups for 50¢, and three chocolate bars and four peanut butter cups for 48¢. What is the most candy (the greatest number of pieces) you can buy for exactly 50¢?

July 31

The digits from 0 to 9 have been used in the multiplication example below (excluding intermediate steps). Fill in the missing numbers.

$$
\begin{array}{r}
\text{x } 0 \ 2 \\
\times \quad \text{x } 9 \\
\hline
1 \ \text{x} \ \text{x} \ \text{x} \ 8 \\
\end{array}
$$

August

The month the Romans originally called Sextilis was re-named August in 27 B.C. for Julius Caesar's adopted son, the first Roman emperor. He was originally named Octavian, but a grateful Senate renamed him Augustus, "revered," after he had managed to kill or defeat all his rivals, including many senators. In a monumental display of modesty, Augustus did not accept the gift until the year 8 B.C.

Try to be outside on clear nights around August 10, the approximate date of a meteor shower that occurs every year. This celestial phenomenon, called the Shower of the Perseids, was noted by the Chaldeans as early as 2700 B.C. The meteors seem to follow the path of a comet through space. Only when they enter our atmosphere do they start to burn up and become visible. It's a beautiful sight!

August 1

Each of these boy's names *except one* can be anagrammed into a common English noun. Which name cannot be made into another word?

CORNELIUS   DANIEL   CAMERON
THOMAS   BOSWELL

August 2

Patty doesn't feel she is really a child anymore. Ten years ago, her mother was five times her age. Now she is three-sevenths of her mother's age, and in five years she will be half her mother's age. How old will she be when she is half her mother's age?

August 3

Shopping can present a terrible dilemma, the new couple discovered. Three pounds of potatoes and two pounds of eggplants cost $2.25. Or they could just buy eggplants for the same amount of money and make a casserole out of all those eggplants. But potatoes are cheaper than eggplants. How much did potatoes cost per pound?

August 4

Can you go from PINK to ROSE in four steps, changing one letter at a time and making a new English word each time?

P	I	N	K
—	—	—	—
—	—	—	—
—	—	—	—
R	O	S	E

August 5

Here a common proverb has been dressed up in multisyllabic guise. Dress it down to its normal language.

A totality of numerous objects that coruscate or are refulgent are not necessarily composed entirely of auriferous substances.

August 6

Find the two anagrams of the same nine letters that make sense in the following statement.

The delegates at the international conference were
extremely _ _ _ _ _ _ _ _ _ .
They had completed the first
_ _ _ _ _ _ _ _ _ agreement in a very
important area, and even though it was not
finalized, it was a good start.

August 7

Each of the following sets of letters has three or more related words interlettered. Unscramble the words, in which all the letters appear in their proper order. (Hint: think food.)

BPKIAINNPEWEAAAINPFCAPRLUEITH

PSPMIEAAZGHTZEBTAATLILS

CPCAURKEADEMDPIUNFGFS

August 8

Mehitabel operated on a peculiar shopping system. She wouldn't allow herself to spend all her money in one place to start, as she had been warned not to do. Therefore, last Saturday she spent half of what she had plus $3.00 at Jones's clothing store, for a blouse; then she spent half of what she had left plus $1.00 at Smith's, and trotted off for stockings to Brown's, where she spent half of what she had left plus $4.00. She was then out of money. How much had she started with?

August 9

These are the dog days of the year. Each of the following words contains the word DOG somewhere. Fill in the missing words.

Persistent, sticking to a goal: __ __ __ __ __ __
A religious theory or belief: __ __ __ __ __
Slang for an old sailor: __ __ __ __ __ __

August 10

The following multiplication example uses all the digits from 0 to 9. Three numbers have been filled in to get you started. Complete the example. (You can use the digits more than once in the intervening steps, but not in the answer.)

$$
\begin{array}{r}
\text{x x x} \\
\text{x 3} \\
\hline
\text{5 x x 0 x}
\end{array}
$$

August 11

The following puzzle is based on the Tom Swifty form, as in, "We lost one of the girls," said Tom ruthlessly. Start at any letter and move up, down, diagonally, or sideways to spell out the message (two null letters to fill up space).

H S Y P A R
W O O A P E
R U L L N T
M T O E L Y
M O M W B B

August 12

Each of these words can be changed into something edible by scrambling the letters and making a new word. How much of a meal can you produce from these anagrams?

PLAYERS   SANDIER   ASSUAGE   BARELY

August 13

On August 13, 1929, a Mr. Perrey crossed the English Channel from Dover to Calais in seven hours and twenty-five minutes on a motorbike equipped with special flotation devices. Can you cross from DAWN to DUSK in only five steps, changing one letter at a time and using a good English word each time?

D	A	W	N
—	—	—	—
—	—	—	—
—	—	—	—
—	—	—	—
D	U	S	K

August 14

Each of the following words contains the letters AUG. Fill in the words.

How we tell the world—and the official—he's on
  the job: _ _ A U G _ _ _ _ _ _
A female offspring: _ A U G _ _ _ _
Unduly proud, rude to the point of arrogance:
                    _ A U G _ _ _
Was visibly and probably audibly amused:
                    _ A U G _ _ _

August 15

The following box will remind you of the weather (at least in the northern hemisphere). Fill in the letters HEAT so that those four letters are in each row, across, down, and on the long diagonal, but no two letters may be the same in any line, nor may two identical letters be next to each other. One line is filled in to get you started.

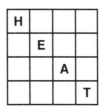

August 16

Our hero the brave knight, is trying to rescue the beautiful Princess of Puzzleland. The maiden has slipped him a message. She will be able to stand at the stable gate from 12:30 to 12:40—but no more than those ten minutes—on the following day. If he arrives promptly, she will elope with him. If not, she will be married later that same evening to his hated rival. The castle is 12 miles away. The first third is uphill, and his horse can make 4 miles per hour uphill; the second third is level, at 8 miles per hour, and the last part, one-third, is downhill, at 12 miles per hour. He figures that that averages out to 8 miles per hour, so if he leaves at 10:55 to give himself five minutes' leeway, he should arrive exactly within the 10 minutes. Of course, he can't get there too early, or he'll be caught hanging around. Does he make it in time? Why or why not?

August 17

The following is an easy type of substitution cryptogram (each letter standing for a different letter—the same substitution each time).

UR   UA   NYXG   RII   GIR   RI   SI
RGWAW   RGUBFA   EUFGR   BIQ

August 18

How many common four-letter English words can you make from the letters EANM using all the letters in each word? Give the words.

August 19

It may look like playing with blocks, but this is a visual puzzle. How many different ways can you form the word COLD? You can use each letter more than once, but you can't use the same combination of letters in a different order. (Letters need not be adjacent.)

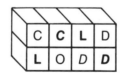

August 20

What number is two-thirds of one-half of one-fourth of 240?

August 21

"See," said the richest man in the world to his secretary as he bought up another country, "money talks." The secretary sighed. "He's right," she said. (The rest is cryptic—a simple substitution.)

"13 15 14 5 25   20 1 12 11 19,   2 21 20
20 15   13 5   9 20   19 1 25 19
7 15 15 4 2 25 5."

August 22

The two youngsters were playing with pennies. Neither of them had many. They did figure out that if you squared the number of Abe's pennies and added Lizzy's pennies, you'd have 62; but if you squared Lizzy's pennies and then added Abe's, you'd have 176 pennies. Since they didn't have either amount, they gave up, but how many pennies did each one actually have?

August 23

All the vowels have been removed from the following statement, and the remaining letters have been broken into groups of three letters each. Replace the vowels and reconstruct the words to read the sentence.

THN	LYT	HNG	WRS	THN	HSB
NDW	HNV	RNT	CSW	HTY	CKR
WHT	YWR	SHS	BND	WHL	WYS
NTC	SWH	TYC	KND	WHT	YWR.

August 24

The name of a country is hidden in each of the following sentences. Find the country.

If you are adventurous, you want a fast boat, but if you just want to be out on the water, a sloop or tug alike will do.

He lost the rally because he got lost on the way, not seeing a semihidden marker.

He opened the window, and, with a loud buzz, air entered the room along with a wasp!

August 25

One word among the following is the odd man out. Which one, and why?

CORSET   COSTER   SECTOR
ESCORT   COURTS

August 26

Sallie Lou likes sequoia trees but not evergreens. She doesn't want either disease, but she'd rather have pneumonia than influenza. She jokes facetiously but not humorously. Does Sallie Lou shop stingily or abstemiously?

August 27

Grandpa was feeling generous, so he gave a total of $100 to his five grandchildren. Starting with the youngest, each got $2.00 more than the next younger one. In other words, the youngest got one sum, the next got $2.00 more, and so on. How much did the youngest grandchild get?

August 28

Jack and John had been friends for a long time—a very long time, it seemed to them. Jack was six years older, but it hadn't made any difference when they met, and it didn't on the day they were talking about their long friendship. "It's twenty-two years this week since we met at Bill's wedding," said John. "Yes, and our ages now, added together, are exactly double what they were then. That makes me feel old," said Jack, but they really were not—not even fifty. How old were they now?

August 29

In each of the word pairs that follows, a different word can be placed between the two words on the line to make two new words. The number of letters is indicated by the dashes. What are the four words?

> BACK _ _ _ _ ROBE
> DOOR _ _ _ STONE
> PAD _ _ _ _ STEP
> SAW _ _ _ _ WHEEL

August 30

What is the five-digit number, with no zeros and no repeated numbers, in which the second digit is two times the first, the third is three times the second, the fourth is four times the first, and the last is one-half more than the second?

August 31

The quotation has been placed in the boxes below and the letters have been put in alphabetical order in the "drop-in" boxes. Word divisions are shown. Fill in the boxes to read the saying. (A dash at the end of a line indicates a broken word.)

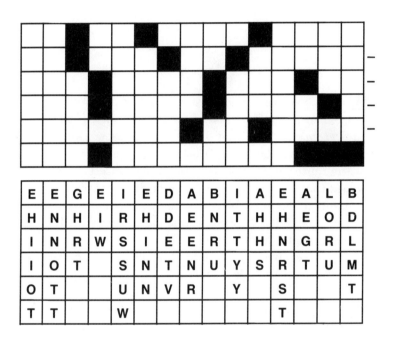

September

A nyone who knows Latin recognizes that the root of September is *septem,* "seven," just as October, November, and December take their names from Roman numbers. However, September is not the seventh month of the year, but the ninth, and it has been the ninth since the Romans decreed that their civic year would start in January in 153 B.C. It did not occur to them that this discrepancy would lead to confusion. After all, people who calculated with Roman numerals would hardly be fazed by such a petty problem. Just try multiplying CVII by XXIV someday when you find yourself with a great deal of time.

The major U.S. holiday in September is Labor Day, the first Monday of the month. It traditionally signals the end of the summer season, as Memorial Day in May signals the beginning. Beaches often close on Labor Day even though swimming can still be very enjoyable. Water changes temperature more slowly than air, so it takes longer to warm up but stays warm longer. Anyone who has swum in the Atlantic in June and September knows that the water is appreciably warmer after Labor Day.

September 1

A palindrome (like Madam I'm Adam) can be words, phrases, or even whole sentences that read the same forward and backward. Work out the following three palindromes.

Legal or illegal ways to obtain something:

— — — — — —   — —   — — —

A description of an Eskimo who has fallen out of his boat: — — — — — — — — —

Look at lots of judges on the sports scene:

— — —   — — — — — — — —

September 2

If you stack the words that match these definitions, you will have a word square that reads the same across and down.

1. Geometric shape
2. Not shut
3. Lack or want
4. Brings to a conclusion, polishes off, finishes

September 3

The following coiled sentence can be unscrambled by finding the right letter for a start, and then tracing letter by letter up, down, sideways, or diagonally to find a statement. (There are two null letters.)

```
I  H  E  W  I  D  R  A
T  T  E  R  I  T  L  Y
D  N  H  S  A  O  N  G
F  O  U  I  M  S  K  I
E  V  I  K  N  H  O  C
```

September 4

Here is a drawing of an unfolded cube, plus six constructed cubes. Which of the drawings *cannot* be made from the unfolded cube at the top?

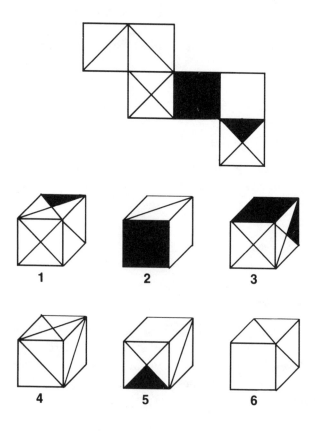

September 5

All the vowels have been removed from the following sentence. (Y is not counted as a vowel.) Put back the vowels to find the sentence. The letters have been broken into groups of 5.

> THRSN   TMSCN   NTHSW   HLPLC
> SDTHC   NDCTR   TNLSS   LYXXX.

September 6

The new teacher thought she'd get the children to drink the milk at recess more cheerfully by offering cookies with it. A lot of the children had illnesses and were out, causing various numbers of children to be present each day. One day the teacher noted that if there were five fewer children the next day, they would each get two cookies more if she brought the same number she had that day. However, the absentee list was low the next day, and she had four more children instead of five fewer. This meant that each received one cookie less than each child had received the day before. How many cookies did the children get the second day?

September 7

The name of a country is hidden in each of the sentences below. Find the countries.

> The doorbell sign said, "Don't touch. In a real emergency, pull the cord."
> They got married secretly, but no one is wed entirely alone, so there were witnesses.
> We needed to visit a health resort, so we went to a spa in another country.

September 8

The circle below contains a word of eight letters with one letter missing. Replace the letter to read the word. It may read counterclockwise, but the letters are in the proper order.

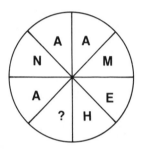

September 9

This problem *must not,* I repeat, *must not* be solved by looking at the telephone. It is a test of your visual memory and your logical ability. Find the sum of all the numbers on a telephone dial and multiply that sum by all the numbers on the telephone dial. What is your answer? (The average time is thirty seconds. Can you beat it?)

September 10

Two names of people are hidden in each sentence below. The letters are in their proper order and are not separated by intervening letters. No name has fewer than three letters. Find the names.

> Oh, call the cab, I'll be ready.
> That tie is all yours, I hate it.
> Get me an orange or get me a lemon, quickly.

September 11

Soon the only trees left with leaves will be pine trees. Can you complete this word square so that the same words can be read across and down? (There can be several answers.)

```
P  I  N  E
I
N
E
```

September 12

There are many words which have the same pair of letters at the beginning and the end, like ONION. Here are four words with only the middle of each one showing. The number of dashes indicates the number of letters that must be placed before and after—the same letters for each individual word, but different letters for different words. Fill in the letters.

     _ _ EPSA _ _   _ _ RISCO _ _
     _ _ IT _ _   _ _ BL _ _

September 13

Each of the following words contains the letters SEP. There may be other appearances of each letter in the word, but each letter is shown only once. Using the definitions, fill in the words.

Architectural term for a church section:
                       _ _ _ _ S E P _
A dangerous occupation working on high locations:
             S _ E _ P _ _ _ _ _ _ _
Put apart: S E P _ _ _ _ _ _

September 14

Just by chance, you run into your dead-beat friend. You lent him $88 some time ago, and haven't seen him (or the money) since. He greets you fondly and says, "Well, it just so happens I have six bills in my pocket that total the $88 I owe you. If you can come up with the denominations of the six bills in thirty seconds, I'll pay you back right now." Spurred on by the only hope of ever seeing your money again, you come up with the six different denominations. What are they?

September 15

Each of the following groups of letters is actually a scrambled word that has had one letter—the same letter for all six words—removed. The remaining letters were then scrambled. Reconstitute the words.

ENCU	RUEC	CATU	RCHA
	IOAR	ANVI	

September 16

In the following mathematics example, you can substitute a different number for each letter (that is, A = the same number each time), and come up with a correct math example.

$$
\begin{array}{r}
A\ B\ C\ D\ E\ F\ G\ H\ I \\
\times\ I \\
\hline
+\ A\ J \\
\hline
A\ A\ A\ A\ A\ A\ A\ A\ A
\end{array}
$$

September 17

A pithy saying has been dropped into the boxes below. Word divisions are indicated and the letters for each of the boxes have been placed, not in their correct order but in alphabetical order, below each column. A dash on the right indicates that a word continues on the next line. Fill in the letters in their proper places in the columns above them to read the statement.

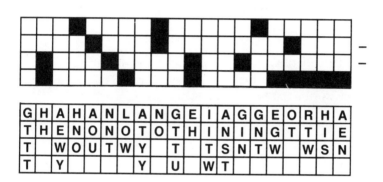

September 18

Can you go from DIRT to ROAD in only seven steps, changing one letter at a time and making a good English word each time? (Example: CAP to HAT—CAP, CAT, HAT)

```
    D    I    R    T
    —    —    —    —
    —    —    —    —
    —    —    —    —
    —    —    —    —
    —    —    —    —
    —    —    —    —
    R    O    A    D
```

September 19

The first word of a word square is given in the diagram below. Fill in the rest, using, in addition to the letters shown, one D, one S, one P, and two each A, E, and T.

L I K E
I
K
E

September 20

One three-letter word can be placed in front of each of the following words to make four new words. The same three-letter word must be used in each case.

_ _ _ BLED
_ _ _ ROW
_ _ _ GIN
_ _ _ TIN

September 21

This brief old-fashioned verse will give you an appropriate word.

My first is in father but not in dad
My second in lass and also lad
My third is in low but not in we
My last in live but not in be
If in my whole no one believes
For thirteen weeks I'll give you leaves.

September 22

The professor posted the grades in the seminar exam (coding them by Social Security number). The student who came in two places below the highest score also came in three places above the poor student who found himself at the bottom of the list. How many students were in the seminar?

September 23

This date marks the birthdate of William McGuffey in 1800. His *Eclectic Readers* sold 122 million copies and taught generations of Americans to read. Can you read this reasonably common word that has been shaped into a square?

```
N  O  C
N     R
I  V  E
```

September 24

The following sentences are missing two words of seven letters each. The same seven letters can be rearranged to make the two missing words.

> The young couple was having trouble fixing a wall, and a visitor said, "I could have told you that you would need _ _ _ _ _ _ _ ." "Oh," said the very much of an amateur young husband, "a piece of grasscloth and a _ _ _ _ _ _ _ won't work?"

September 25

The following multisyllabic pronouncement is a badly garbled proverb. Translate it into common English.

Individuals residing in habitations composed of dried vegetable matter are seriously advised to consider the inadvisability of having seats of power kept for safekeeping in a repository in said domicile.

September 26

I lost my wallet, and I don't remember how much money I had, but I remember thinking the first time I bought something that it cost 10 percent of what I had. Then I noticed that the second purchase was also exactly 10 percent of what I had left. My sales slips totaled $19. How much was in the wallet when I lost it?

September 27

We have a slow set of trains here. One train runs from A to B at 19 miles per hour. The other runs from B to A at 21 miles per hour (it's a slightly improved model). One hour before the trains pass each other, how far apart are they?

September 28

The two youngsters were given different amounts for their allowances. This week, the older received 40¢ plus one-half the total of the younger's allowance. The younger one got 20¢ plus half again as much. The two together received 85¢. How much did each of them have?

September 29

The youngsters decided to spend their weekly allowance on bubble gum. In addition to their 85¢, they managed to dig up $1.31 from under a sofa cushion. If the pieces of bubble gum had been one cent cheaper each, they would have received three more pieces of bubble gum than they did. How many pieces did they actually get?

September 30

Using the numbers 0, 4, 8, and 12 in the following square, you can complete it so that all the vertical, horizontal, and long diagonal rows add up to 24. (You may use each number more than once.)

0		12	0
4			
			12

October

The October Revolution that brought the Bolsheviks to power in Russia actually took place on November 7, 1917, according to most history books. This confusion has its roots in a slight error in Julius Caesar's calculations, which caused his calendar to fall slowly behind the seasons. By the time of Pope Gregory XIII, dates were once again confused. In 1582, Gregory decreed that October 5–14 should be dropped from that year, and that every fourth year should be a Leap Year *except* for centenary years that are *not* divisible by 400 (e.g., 1800). Dropping ten days produced considerable dismay in the countries that were affected. Many people were absolutely convinced that Gregory had chopped ten days off their life!

The non-Catholic countries of Europe ignored the new Gregorian calendar until the pressure of being "behind" the rest of the world grew too great. England and its colonies finally accepted the new calendar in 1752, skipping September 3–13. Russia maintained the old Julian calendar into the twentieth century. Only after the Revolution, which occurred on October 26, 1917 (Julian style), did the Russians "catch up" with the rest of the world.

October 1

The school faculty is conducting a prize drawing to raise money for Mensa memberships for bright students. You have to pick the tickets out of a box that looks like a dictionary. There are fifteen nonprizewinning slips, ten $1.00 winners, and five slips that are worth $25 each. How much would you have to spend at $1.00 per ticket to be sure of winning one of the $25 prizes?

October 2

Make as many common English words as you can from the letters ECRTU using each of the letters only once in each word. (Many people found five or more.)

October 3

Each of the words shown below contains the letters OCT. Definitions are given and the number of letters is shown for each. Fill in the words.

A form of firework: _ _ _ _ O C _ _ T
A form of marine life: O C T _ _ _ _
A soup: _ O C _ T _ _ _ _ _

October 4

The famous mathematician Dr. Square Root had two sons, exactly a year apart. One day, shortly after they had both turned a year older, he noticed that if you squared their ages and then added the squares the total would be 1105. How old were his sons?

October 5

One of the marks of creativity is seeing associations. The following list of words should call to mind other words using this word, whether as part of a word, or part of a phrase, or just in a related manner. (Example: TAG—tagalong, tag out, ragtag) Four each will earn you full credit.

WAIST
SPOT
LOVE
CHECK

October 6

The field shown below belonged to a rancher. Twelve oil wells were drilled on it. The rancher, who had four sons, left them the field, divided into four equal sections, each with three oil wells on it. Divide the land so that each has an identical share, and every plot has square corners.

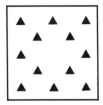

October 7

The same seven letters, if rearranged into two words, will make sense of the following sentence.

Said the angry husband, "I'm leaving. We are
_ _ _ _ _ _ _ . I cannot put up with your
ceaseless gabble and _ _ _ _ _ _ _ ."

October 8

We're between fall and winter at the moment, but can you change FALL to COLD in five steps, using a good English word each time? (Example: CAT to DOG—CAT COT COG DOG) Slang words don't count.

F A L L

— — — —

— — — —

— — — —

— — — —

C O L D

October 9

Lost in Liars and Truthtellers Town, you are in real trouble. You need to ask directions from a Truthteller, but how can you tell who is a Truthteller? You stop a group of three women and ask if they are Truthtellers. The first says, "Two of us are Truthtellers." The second says, "Only one of us is a Truthteller." And the third one chimes in, "The last woman who spoke is telling the truth." Well, who was or were Truthtellers?

October 10

It was the middle of the winter in Scandinavia, and the poor boy, sick with a cold, was lying in bed. He woke up in the night, but he knew that the night lasted from 3:00 P.M. to 9:00 A.M. at that time of year. The boy wearily glanced at his clock and, thinking it said 4:42, buried his head back in the pillow. But as he fell asleep he realized he hadn't distinguished the hour hand from the minute hand. If it wasn't 4:42 in the morning, what other time (or times) could it have been?

October 11

The following visual puzzle has been set up so that each of the signs has a numerical value. The sum of each row and column except one is shown. Figure out the missing number.

⊗	👥	⬦	☎	110
👥	⊗	⬦	☎	110
👥	☎	⬦	⊗	110
⊗	👥	☎	⬦	110
90	**105**	**125**	**?**	

October 12

If 7 is a prime number, cross out all the A's and E's below; if not, cross out the C's and L's. If the square root of 625 is 25, cross out the I's and R's; if not, cross out the C's and U's. If 0°C and 10°F are the same, cross out the B's, M's, and S's; if not, cross out the X's. What do you have left?

C A O X L E U E M I B R U X S E

October 13

Since this is the day after Columbus discovered America, here's a Columbus puzzle. Sum the digits of the year in which Columbus reached the New World. Add to that the number of the king whom Mary, Ferdinand and Isabella's daughter, married. Add the number of ships in Columbus's fleet, and divide by 3. What do you have?

October 14

I met my friend the test pilot, who had just received a lot of publicity for a record round-the-world flight by balloon. With the pilot was a little girl of about two. "What's her name?" I asked my friend, whom I hadn't seen in five or six years and who had married in that time. "Same as her mother." "Hello, Susan," I said. How did I know if I had never seen the wedding announcement?

October 15

Start with the letter A. Add the letters below in order, making a new word each step, until you make a seven-letter word. Adding an S to make a plural is not allowed; you must rearrange the letters or add a letter to make a completely new word. (Example: I, it, tin, tine)

R   E   C   S   S   T

October 16

The weary clothing merchant was cleaning up after his Columbus week coat sale. He had already marked the coats down twice, but he still had one nice coat for sale. It had originally been $300. At the first markdown, he had reduced it to $210. At the second markdown, for Columbus week, he had tagged it at $147. If he marks it down now on the same principle, what will the new price be?

October 17

What is the four-digit number, no zeros, in which the first number is five times the last, the second is four more than the first and three times the third, and the third is two more than the last and two less than the first?

October 18

Of the three finalists in the science scholarship contest, John, William, and Sally came in one, two, and three, but not necessarily in that order. The winner was the physicist. The one who was not last or first was the mathematician. The one who came in last had black hair. John had brown hair. Sally had red hair. John did not have any training in physics. Who was first?

October 19

George Bernard Shaw said that fish could be spelled *ghoti* (*gh* as in rough, *o* as in women, and *ti* as in nation). Can you come up with the longest way of spelling SIGH, following the same idea?

October 20

People have already started buying Halloween candy, the better to eat before Halloween. Our local candy store was selling large sacks of candy for 25¢ and small sacks for 10¢. The new cashier wasn't up to the job, though; she marked down the number of sacks she sold, but she forgot to record their prices. At the end of the day she found she had sold 385 candy sacks and had $62.65 in her cash register. Before her boss came by, however, she figured out how many of each size of candy sack she had sold. Can you?

October 21

Palindromes are words, phrases or sentences reading the same backward as forward, like Madam I'm Adam. Here are some palindrome definitions. Fill in the palindromes. (One word is given in each to get you started.)

Some confusion about a vehicle or an animal in sight:

_ _ _   _ _   _   C A R   _ _

_   _ _ _   _   _ _ _ ?

Roy didn't like the big city at all and wouldn't stay.

_ _ _   _ _ _   _ _ _ _ _ ,

_ _ _   WENT   _ _ .

October 22

A simple magic square is easy. It's a square in which all the numbers from 1 to 9, placed in a grid as shown below, add up to 15 in each direction. Make an anti-magic square, in which each line total—across, down, and long diagonals—is different.

Magic Square

4	9	2
3	5	7
8	1	6

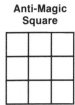

Anti-Magic Square

October 23

It's difficult being called on unexpectedly in class, but Professor Jones decided to do it to wake up his sleeping students. "I don't mind if you know my age," he said. "It's in all the directories, and I can assume the approximate age of one of you. No written homework tonight for the first person who can solve this: If you subtract one age from mine, you'll get 44, but if you multiply them together, you'll get 1280." It took Tom fifteen seconds, because he tried his age in the problem, and it was right. How old were Tom and the professor?

October 24

The spider web shown below contains eight words. Each section contains four letters which have been jumbled. They all contain one missing letter, which should be placed in the box with the question mark. Figure out the missing letter, and reassemble the eight words.

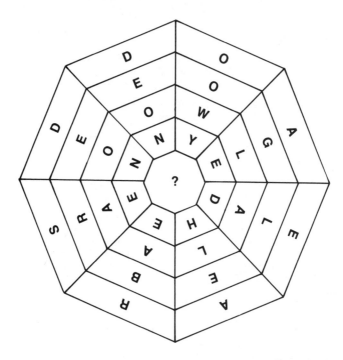

October 25

Sometimes it helps to be bigger—especially when you're only four or five years old. The children were making candy apples for the Halloween party, eating as they worked. The bigger kids managed to gobble up seven apples apiece (and got stomachaches for their pains), but the little kids got only two apiece. The children managed to eat twenty-four apples among them. How many kids, big and small, were making the candy apples?

October 26

A rather softhearted antique dealer often paid more than she should and sold for less than she could. This time, she was figuring out her costs and profits. Her sister said, "You sold that dish for only a 5 percent profit. If you had bought it for 10 percent less than you did pay, and sold it at the same price, you would have made a $15 profit." How much did the antique dealer pay for the dish?

October 27

Sheila, buying favors for a party she was giving, was having difficulty deciding on how many more favors to buy. She started out by planning to give everyone three favors, but when she divided the favors she had by 3, she had one left over; when she divided by 4, she had two left over; by 5, she had three left over; and by 6, she had four left over. Since she was going to have ten guests, this wouldn't work. She counted the favors and realized that, by adding two more, she could divide the favors evenly. What is the smallest number of favors she could already have bought to meet those specifications?

October 28

Another word to guess letter by letter.

> My first is in water but not in tears
> My second in listen but not in hears
> My third in three but not in she
> My fourth in clear but not in tea
> My last in hang but not in grand
> My whole assembles in a band.

October 29

A word square is a square in which words read the same across and down.

Example: C A T
A T E
T E A

Make up a four-letter-by-four-letter word square in which you use five E's, four N's, two M's, two each, A and D, and one S.

October 30

This may be an old one, but many people seem not to have heard it. Samantha and Suzy were squabbling over a small cake. Their mother solved the question of which one should cut it, as well as the problem of how to make sure the pieces were even, in a very simple manner. No one could complain. What was her solution?

October 31

This being Halloween, we will consider the problem of witches and their cats. The whole crowd is out tonight, naturally, and an interested observer, seeing them fly by (yes, witches' cats fly), noticed that the number of legs, all told, was three and a half times the number of heads, and the total of heads and legs was seventy-two. How many cats and witches are out this Halloween?

November

November starts with All Saints' Day. This holiday dates back to the seventh century, when the Pantheon, which means "all saints," was dedicated by Pope Boniface IV in Rome. In many countries All Saints' remains the traditional day for remembering the dead with visits to the cemetery and the placing of flowers on tombs. In our country, however, this holiday has been overshadowed by All Hallows' Eve, "All Souls' Evening," the night before, when supernatural spirits are supposed to be abroad. We now know October 31 as Halloween.

Since 1941, the fourth Thursday of November has been the date to observe Thanksgiving. This peculiarly American holiday celebrates the survival of the colony at Plymouth, Massachusetts, after many hardships. Turkey, cranberry sauce, and succotash, all strictly North American foods, have become traditional. It is not generally realized that when the Pilgrims landed, they were greeted by an English-speaking native named Squanto. It must have been a shock for the Pilgrims to hear him—and it seems to be a shock for people to hear about him now. Squanto had already been taken to England by whalers and fishermen plying the North American coast.

November 1

Up north, November is not too early for snow. Fill the square below with the letters SNOW. Each line down, sideways, and along the diagonals must contain each of the four letters, though their order is not important. Three letters have been inserted to give you a start.

S			N
		S	

November 2

The following is a simple substitution cryptogram in which a number has been substituted for a letter. The same number stands for the same letter each time.

26   25 18 9 23   18 13   7 19 22
19 26 13 23   18 8   14 22 8 8 2.

November 3

The poor knight who is madly in love with the beautiful Princess of Puzzleland is ready to elope again. He missed his princess once because of his bad math. This time he has it right. He's figured out exactly how fast he must go to reach the castle exactly at noon when she will slip out. If he goes at 75 miles per hour in his brand-new twelve-elf-powered Magicmobile, and leaves at 7:00 A.M., he'll get there an hour too soon. On the other hand, if he goes at a steady 50 miles per hour, he'll be an hour too late, he finds. How fast must he tell his lead elf to travel to reach his intended bride just on time?

November 4

The wicked witch of Puzzleland, angered by three Liars from the under-30 set, told each of them how much longer he was going to live. The witch said, "You have a total of 130 years left among you. The oldest has already lived half his life; the second oldest has lived one third; and the youngest, who told me more lies than anyone else, has already lived one third of his life." How old were the Liars?

November 5

The phrase coiled below is rather unusual and not just because it has (unintended) political overtones. If you start at the correct letter, and move to any letter, up, down, diagonally, or sideways, you can read the phrase.

```
S  A  D  Y  Y  T  S
T  R  E  B  D  A  R
C  O  M  E  M  O  C
```

November 6

Each of the following words contains the letters NOV. (There may be more than one of each of those letters, but they are not shown.) Using the definitions, fill in the words.

A dispute or argument:

_ _ N _ _ O V _ _ _ _

An astronomical feature:

_ _ _ _ _ N O V _

New or original: _ _ N O V _ _ _ _ _

November 7

What is the four-digit number in which the first digit is one-fourth of the last digit, the second digit is 6 times the first digit, and the third digit is the second digit plus 3?

November 8

Five letters can be rearranged for *each pair* of words below to match the two definitions. A different set of five letters is used for each line.

To toss; the value of
To perch; part of the human body
One who looks; feed on meadow grass, etc.

November 9

Another palindrome set of definitions—the word or phrase will read the same backward and forward (Example: First man introduces himself—Madam I'm Adam)

The big chiefs are showing grief:

— — — — — —   — — —

A person who lives in a city in Nevada and tends to
be solitary: — — — —   — — — — —

November 10

All the vowels have been removed from the following remark, and the letters have been broken into groups of three. Replace the missing vowels (one null letter at end).

FLS RSH NWH RNG LSF RTT RDX.

November 11

A solemn holiday like Veterans Day really isn't the subject for a joke or humor, but test your memory of the day. The two interlettered lines below contain names in the first line, and places in the second, relating to World War I and World War II.

P F C E O H R C U S H H R C I H N I L G L

B E Y A L P S A R T L E O A M S G E N I E N

November 12

A group of youngsters found a large sum of money on the street and took it to the police. The grateful owner gave each of them a reward. If there had been two more youngsters in the group, they each would have received $1.00 less, with $2.00 left over to be divided into cents. If there had been double the number, each would have received exactly $2.50 less. If there had been three fewer of them, each one would have received $2.00 more and there would have been $1.00 left to split into pennies. This way, each received an exact sum in dollars, with no cents left over. How many youngsters and how large a reward for each?

November 13

Divide 110 into two parts so that one will be 150 percent of the other. What are the 2 numbers?

November 14

The following matchsticks make one triangle. Rearrange five of them to make 5 triangles.

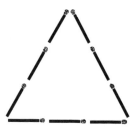

November 15

As Amy was strolling one day with her baby daughter in her carriage, she met her husband's mother's only daughter-in-law's sister's husband. What relationship was this man to Amy?

November 16

A word square is composed of four words that read the same across and down. The first word of the square below has been filled in for you. Make up a word square, using this as a start, in which you use, in total, four E's; two each, S, O, L, and D; and one each, A and P.

```
S  O  L  E
O
L
E
```

November 17

Can you go from GLOW to WORM in only seven steps, changing one letter at a time and making a good English word at each step?

G	L	O	W
—	—	—	—
—	—	—	—
—	—	—	—
—	—	—	—
—	—	—	—
W	O	R	M

November 18

Another Victorian-type poem in which the correct letter from each clue gives you a new word.

> My first is in ocean but not in sea
> My second in milk but not in me
> My third in three but not in throw
> My fourth in vow but not in crow
> My fifth in eight but not in night
> My last in wrong and also right
> My whole is praise for thoughts or men
> Or women, too, or tongue or pen.

November 19

Your pockets are tearing from the weight of all the coins in them. After you unload them onto the kitchen table, you discover something surprising. You have exactly the same number of pennies, nickels, dimes, and quarters, totaling $6.15. How many of each coin do you have?

November 20

Sally likes things with certain characteristics. She likes apples but not pears. She likes beets but not turnips. She likes beef but not lamb. Does she like cheese or custard, and why?

November 21

Gabe was having a terrible time lining up his tin soldiers. He didn't have all that many, fewer than one hundred, but he couldn't seem to arrange them on parade properly. He kept having odd numbers left over. He tried rows of five and there were four left over; he tried rows of six—four left over; rows of 7—one left over. He finally decided to have a very narrow parade and arranged them four abreast. That worked. What's the smallest number of toy soldiers he could have had?

November 22

Still wandering in Liars and Truthtellers Town, you run into two women, but cannot tell if either tells the truth. You ask the first one, "Is either of you a Truthteller?" After she answers, you know the truth. What did she say?

November 23

You've almost finished renovating the storage room in the basement, but find you are short two panels and send your young son out to buy one oak panel and one plain. He comes back with the panels and change, so you can tell he spent $65.15, but he's lost the sales slip, and you don't know what each cost. All he can remember is that the oak panel cost $5.45 more than the plain one. What did each panel cost?

November 24

Today may not be Thanksgiving, but it's an appropriate time for a Thanksgiving puzzle. A pertinent message has been dropped into the boxes below. Word divisions are indicated by black boxes, and the letters for each of the boxes have been placed, not in correct order but in alphabetical order, below each column. Fill in the letters in their proper places in the columns above them to read the message. A dash represents a broken word.

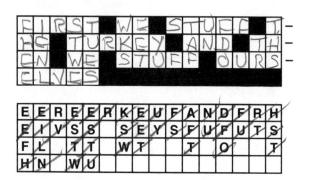

November 25

If you haven't heard this one before, good. If you have, our apologies, but it's so clever we had to include it. After a heavy Thanksgiving meal, the night watchman went to work. In the morning, he told his boss he had dreamed that a saboteur planted a bomb in the factory and that he felt it was a warning. The boss promptly fired him. Why?

November 26

You are on your way home for the holidays with the family. You fill the gas tank of your nice new small car, which holds 10 gallons and gives you 25 miles to the gallon. That should get you home easily, as home is 220 miles away. Unfortunately, about 20 miles from home, the car stops, and you discover the tank is dry—obviously a leak, because you can see drops dripping. How many gallons of gasoline have you lost? (And although it is not part of the question, what will you say to the new car dealer who just sold you the car?)

November 27

The following statement has been coiled. If you start at the right letter and move in any direction, you can come up with a Tom Swifty.

```
W  I  T  C  R  U
C  E  P  H  H  C
A  Y  R  S  E  H
L  R  A  E  R  T
L  C  O  I  U  E
Y  M  T  D  N  D
```

November 28

What are three single digits whose sum is the same as that of the digits multiplied?

November 29

The following words contain some unusual letter combinations. Fill in the missing letters.

_ Y N A _ _   _ W K W _ _ _
_ Y Z Y _ _

November 30

The family had missed the plane back home and all its members were very irritated. "Oh well," said the older boy, "if it were six hours later, we'd only have to wait one-fifth as long until midnight, when the plane comes, as we'd have to wait if it were two hours earlier now." Figuring that out helped pass the time. What time was it?

December

In much of the country, December can be recognized by the Christmas decorations. Lights and ornaments go up immediately after Thanksgiving. (In France, I've seen them up as early as November 12, right after Armistice Day.) Actually, most of these trappings date back to pre-Christian times. The Christmas tree is a relic of ancient tree worship. The custom of decorating such a tree was brought to England from Germany by Queen Victoria's husband, Prince Albert, and it spread to the United States from there. "The Holly and the Ivy" are both Druid symbols.

Even the date of Christmas was not set until sometime in the third century, and it was probably chosen to be near the winter solstice, around December 21. Many people already celebrated a festival on that day to bring back the sun after the longest night of the year. Even now, exchanging gifts on Christmas Day is actually peculiar to the English-speaking world. Other cultures use different dates, the most common being January 6. That would give people a little more time to finish their shopping!

December 1

Each of the following words contains the letters DEC once, if not twice.

Not sedate or proper:
$$\_ \_ \text{D E C} \_ \_ \_ \_ \_$$
A statistical term:
$$\text{D E C} \_ \_ \_$$
Ornamented, often used for overornamented:
$$\_ \_ \text{D E C} \_ \_ \_$$

December 2

A word square is composed of four words that read the same across as down. The first word of the following square has been filled in for you. Complete the square with the missing three words using five E's; four N's; two each M, A, D; and one S, in total (16 letters for the complete square).

M A N E
A
N
E

December 3

You can, if you want to waste a lot of time, count sheep by counting heads and legs and dividing by 5. However, could you figure out how many birds (two-legged) and how many mammals (four-legged) your local zoo had? You counted 78 legs and 35 heads. How many of each were there?

December 4

It was one of those silly guessing games for a prize. How many Christmas tree balls were in the big bowl in the department store? Surprisingly, there were only five guesses. Jim was five under, Susan was two under, Willy was the winner, Jack was one over, and Alice was six over. The numbers were: 26, 15, 18, 21, and 20. How many ornaments were in the bowl?

December 5

The old lady who lived in a shoe was having some real trouble buying Christmas presents for her enormous family. Although she bought the least expensive stocking stuffers she could find, the bill was high. Of course, both a 15 percent sales tax and a 5 percent luxury tax were added to the original price. She paid a total of $100. What was the cost of the stuffers before taxes?

December 6

The farmers were bringing their fowl to market to sell for Christmas dinner, all nicely frozen, of course. Farmer Jones had three plump, nice fowl and had managed to simplify her pricing by getting them all to the identical weight. Farmer Smith had geese, four of them, and he, too, had all of them at the same weight, which was different from that of Farmer Jones's birds. Three fowl from Farmer Jones and four fowl from Farmer Smith weighed 38 pounds. On the other hand, if Farmer Jones had had four fowl and Farmer Smith had had three, the combined weight would have been 39 pounds. How much did each of Farmer Jones's fowl weigh?

December 7

An illuminating statement has been inserted into the boxes as shown. The letters comprising the statement are below their appropriate location, but in alphabetical order. Dashes indicate word breaks. Put the letters in their proper places to read the message.

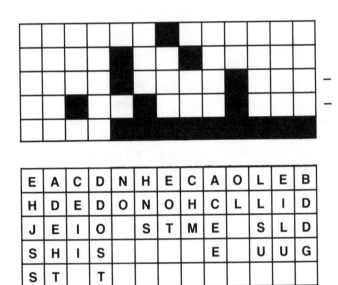

December 8

The following sentence is missing two words composed of the same six letters. Find the two words composed of the same six letters that will make (reasonable) sense in this puzzle.

The versatile dance team could, in a

— — — — — — , switch from a waltz to a

— — — — — — .

December 9

A palindrome is a word, phrase, sentence, or line that can be read backward or forward. (Example: First man to first woman, Madam I'm Adam) Here are two palindrome descriptions to figure out. Letter divisions are shown.

Instruction to someone who is afraid, in a gun duel:

— — — —   —   — — — — — —

All the inhabitants of ancient Rome were smart, not stupid: __ __   __ __ __ __ __   __

— — — — —

December 10

Each of the lines below has a blank space between the two words. Find a letter that can replace the first letter in each pair of words to make two new words and put it on that line. When you have finished, if you do it correctly, you will have a new word, reading down.

CHOP	_____	HAVING
AIL	_____	PURSE
AVER	_____	AIL
FOUND	_____	BRIGHT

December 11

"Aha," said the math professor to her husband, "it's a very simple problem, but I see that our two sons have now reached interesting ages. The product of their ages is six times the amount you get if you add their ages. On the other hand, if you add the square of each age, the total of the two will be 325." How old were their boys?

December 12

One letter has been left out of the center of this scrambled words puzzle. If you take each of the letters in the sections reading down toward the center, rearrange them, and add the missing letter from the middle, you will have eight different five-letter words. Fill in the missing letter and unscramble the words.

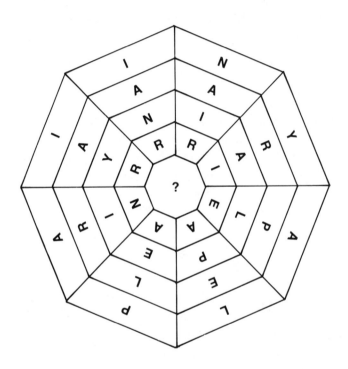

December 13

The Wantsits were going to buy a used, but serviceable car. Mr. Wantsits was quite upset. He said he had seen one he liked but it was $6950, and they couldn't afford that much. At least, that's what he thought it cost. His wife had been shopping around and was pretty sure that she had seen one for $4575. As it turned out, both of them had faulty memories and were wrong by the identical amount; one was over and one was under. They had been looking at the same car! What did it really cost?

December 14

Johnny, despite his mother's objections, spent his whole allowance of $2.16 ($2.00, with 16¢ left from last week) on bubble gum. If the pieces of gum had been a penny cheaper, he would have received three more pieces than he did. How many did he actually buy?

December 15

Find a five-digit number in which the last number is the sum of the first, second, and third; the third is four less than the last; the fourth is two less than the last; and the first and fourth added are one less than the last. The last number is also three times the second.

December 16

You have an appointment to meet your friend the logic professor during the winter holidays when she is on vacation. Today is Friday. She has told you to meet her two days after the day before the day after tomorrow. What day does she expect you?

December 17

The combined ages of Jim and his daughter total thirty-one. Jim is exactly thirty years older than his daughter. How old is his daughter?

December 18

At the Winter Carnival, you see a new ring-toss game on sale. There are five rings, numbered 16, 17, 23, 24, and 39. You can use each ring as many times as you want to reach the score that is picked for each game. While you are watching, the salesman chooses 100, and dares the crowd to pick the smallest combination of ring tosses that will give that score. Naturally, you win. What rings did you pick?

December 19

By changing one letter at a time, can you go from GRASS to GREEN in seven steps, making a good English word at each step? Fill in the word ladder below.

$$
\begin{array}{ccccc}
G & R & A & S & S \\
\_ & \_ & \_ & \_ & \_ \\
\_ & \_ & \_ & \_ & \_ \\
\_ & \_ & \_ & \_ & \_ \\
\_ & \_ & \_ & \_ & \_ \\
\_ & \_ & \_ & \_ & \_ \\
\_ & \_ & \_ & \_ & \_ \\
G & R & E & E & N
\end{array}
$$

December 20

Santa had hired extra workers for the packing process. He really didn't know quite how many he would need, so he watched his new workers for a while. He found out that six elves could pack eighteen packages in half an hour. How many packages could twelve elves pack in ninety minutes?

December 21

You're stumbling through the forest at the edge of Liars and Truthtellers Town. In the dark you bump into a man. "Who are you?" you ask wearily. "I'm a Liar," he replies. What have you learned?

NOTE: Winter's back, and so are some old favorites. The remaining ten puzzles are special. Each is an "oldie but goody" disguised in a slightly different garb. Some of them will probably be new to you. None is original, but each has been fooling and delighting readers for many years. The percentage of correct responses has been omitted from the answers.

December 22

The following diagram is one I remember from my high school math class. You must draw one continuous, curving line (in two dimensions) that passes through every single line segment in the diagram at one point, and one point only, not along the line. Can you solve it?

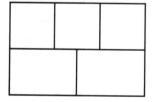

December 23

My colleague, in addition to being intelligent, witty, and a fine dancer, has long red hair and blue eyes. Everybody in the office except the boss is under thirty; I'm twenty-five. I am young, male, single and unattached, and not particularly shy. I happen to be attracted to women with long red hair and blue eyes, but I have never complimented my colleague or suggested that we go out on a date. Why not?

December 24

My friend is coming to share Christmas Eve with me. I live on the fifteenth floor. Unfortunately, he arrives without being announced by the doorman, puffing and panting from walking the last five flights. When he leaves, however, he gets into the elevator for the ride down. How can this be?

December 25

We are going home for Christmas Day. I note that it takes us two and a half hours to get there because of the terrible traffic. The traffic is just as bad on the way home—identical, in fact—but we make it in 150 minutes. How do we manage this trick?

December 26

Daddy gave his three boys the same present—money. He gave them $17 and, being a bit of a practical joker, said, "The oldest gets one-half the money, the middle one gets one-third of the money, and the baby gets one-ninth. However, it must be in even dollars." How did the boys solve that one?

December 27

My brother started out from Boston, and I started out from New York, to meet in New Haven for lunch. When we met in New Haven, which of us was farther from Boston?

December 28

Your aged grandmother tells you she was born on February 29, 1900. How old is she as of the date you are doing this puzzle?

December 29

How many 9's do you pass when you start at 1 and count up to 100?

December 30

It's a mistake to hire amateurs, as the archaeologist found to his great distress. One of his new staff came running in one day, all excited. He had just paid a local a great deal of money for an extremely valuable coin. As he said, "I've never seen one like this before, and I've been looking in museums for thirty years. It's a genuine Egyptian coin marked 100 B.C.—solid gold!" The director of the expedition sighed wearily and fired him. Why?

December 31

Joe said to his friend, "It's really surprising. Yesterday I was twenty, but next year I'll be twenty-two." How could Joe make that statement without lying?

Answers

Day 1 of Each Month

January: WAS IT A RAT I SAW? and DESSERTS I STRESSED. (79%)

February: TEN ANIMALS I SLAM IN A NET; STAR BRATS. Only 20% of the Mensa members found both palindromes, though 95% found the latter.

March: The correct answer is (a) 9 1. There are two series, one starting with 10 and going down one number each time, and one starting with 1 and going up one number. (98%)

April: You'd call her Sally or Lorraine or Chun-Li or whatever her name was. This is an impossible relationship to figure out. Only 15 percent of the Mensans spotted the April Fools' Day joke. The rest had many names to call *me*.

May: SPRING (75%)

June: PERMUTATION is the only permutation of the word IMPORTUNATE. (55%)

July: Jim (65%)

August: CORNELIUS can be anagrammed to RECLUSION; DANIEL to DENIAL (and NAILED); CAMERON to ROMANCE and CREMONA; and BOSWELL TO BELLOWS. Only THOMAS cannot be rearranged. (75%)

September: BORROW OR ROB; DEKAYAKED; SEE REFEREES (85%)

October: The cost of winning a $25 ticket for certain is $26. Of course, you're certain to win more than $25 with that investment. (85%)

November: This was the most common solution. (65%)

S	O	W	N
N	W	O	S
O	S	N	W
W	N	S	O

December: INDECOROUS; DECILE; BEDECKED (85%)

Day 2 of Each Month

January: A mango costs 15¢. The "logic" is 3¢ per letter (that's the way stores in Puzzleland operate). (73%)

February: A FOOL AND HIS MONEY ARE SOON PARTED. (98%)

March: ATTACK AT DAWN MONDAY. The lieutenant read the first letter of each word. (100%)

April: NEEDS and DENSE are the missing words. (100%)

May: Nineteen hundred eighty pennies are worth one cent more than 1979 pennies, just as ten pennies are worth one cent more than nine pennies. (80%)

June: PEDESTRIANS COME IN TWO SORTS: THE QUICK AND THE DEAD. (75%)

July: There are four girls and three boys. (70%)

August: She will be twenty. (75%)

September: (80%)

```
C  O  N  E
O  P  E  N
N  E  E  D
E  N  D  S
```

October: CRUET, CURET, CUTER, ERUCT, RECUT, and TRUCE were all found. Ninety-five percent of the Mensa members found four anagrams, and 55 percent found five.

November: A BIRD IN THE HAND IS MESSY. Number the alphabet backward from 26. (80%)

December: (85%)

```
M  A  N  E
A  M  E  N
N  E  E  D
E  N  D  S
```

Day 3 of Each Month

January: CATASTROPHE; CAT BURGLAR; CATALOGUE (100%)

February: IT KEEPS YOUR NECK OFF THE LINE. (95%)

March: The solution favored by 60 percent of the Mensans was:

Another 30 percent gave:

Give yourself credit for either, or for one of your own.

April: CAMEL; ELAND; SEAL (90%)

May: RENO; BARRE; BUTTE (90%)

June: HAPPINESS IS A STOCK THAT SPLITS THREE FOR ONE THE DAY AFTER YOU BUY IT. This cryptogram could be figured out through word structure and trial and error, or you could simply look at the characters on a typewriter. Each letter was replaced with the one to its right on the standard Qwerty keyboard. (65%)

July: (40%)

$$\begin{array}{r} 396 \\ \underline{45} \\ 17820 \end{array}$$

August: Potatoes are 25¢. Eggplants are 75¢. (35%)

September: "I THINK I'VE FOUND THE WIRE," SAID TOM SHOCKINGLY. Start at the top left letter. (90%)

October: SKYROCKET; OCTOPUS; MOCK TURTLE (95%)

November: Sixty miles per hour will do it. (75%)

December: Thirty-one birds and four mammals (65%)

Day 4 of Each Month

January: Margot likes unknown writers. She only likes words with a silent letter. (60%)

February: The word is HAND. (100%)

March: LLOYD for a boy, DOLLY for a girl (98%)

April: Women equal 23–15–13–5–14. The numbers represent the position of each letter of the word in the alphabet: i.e., A = 1, B = 2, and so on. (70%)

May: TSGSI. This is a substitution cipher which has to be worked letter by letter. (60%)

June: Only 40 percent of the Mensans surveyed tried this puzzle, but all those who did got it right.

214	219	254	259
659	654	619	614
873	873	873	873

July: If you answered every question right, you were left with INDEPENDENCE. (95%)

August: PINK, PINE, PONE, POSE, ROSE is one solution. (100%)

September: Cube 5 cannot be made from the unfolded one. Only 30 percent of the Mensans got this one right. Three of those confessed they had photocopied the drawing and folded it themselves. That's not cheating—that's using all your resources.

October: Twenty-three and twenty-four (60%)

November: Their ages were 28, 26, and 25. Only 40% of the Mensans who took it got this one.

December: Twenty (95%)

Day 5 of Each Month

January: Twenty hours (96%)

February: Nine puzzle makers. Each puzzler can compose one puzzle per day. (75%)

March: TIMID, I'M IT. Only 65 percent of the Mensans got this one correct. Several said that either you see palindromes or you don't. Those who do love them.

April: The package will cost 5¢. If, as many people assume, the package cost 10¢ and the widget cost $1.00, then their total cost would be more than $1.10. (75%)

May: NUPTIALS (95%)

June: Ann is four years old now. (80%)

July: Your question was, "Would the other person tell me that this apple is all right to eat?" If the person is the Truthteller and the apple is fine, she'll say, "No," because that's what the Liar would say. If the person is the Liar and the apple is fine, she'll say, "No," because that's *not* what the Truthteller would say. Similarly, if the apple will put you to sleep, the person will have to say "Yes." Only 40 percent got this one.

August: All that glitters is not gold. (85%)

September: "THERE ISN'T A MUSICIAN IN THIS WHOLE PLACE," SAID THE CONDUCTOR TONELESSLY. (65%)

October: WAIST appears in SHIRTWAIST, WAISTBAND, WAIST-COAT, WAISTLINE, and other words. SPOT is in SPOT CHECK, SPOT ON, SPOTLIGHT, HOT SPOT, and RUN SPOT RUN. LOVE helps to make up LOVEBIRD, LOVESONG, LOVELIGHT, PUPPY LOVE, TRUE LOVE, and more. CHECK is the root of CHECK-MATE, CHECK OUT, CHECK UP, CHECKBOOK, BED CHECK, and CHECKERED. Give yourself full credit if you found four associations for each word. (40%)

November: STAR COMEDY BY DEMOCRATS. You can start either at the upper left or the upper right, since this phrase is a palindrome. (70%)

December: $83.33. The taxes are 20 percent of the *selling* price. (65%)

Day 6 of Each Month

January: Cressida is four years old. (64%)

February: There were half a dozen different ways to make this move. The most common was POOR, POOL, POLL, POLE, PILE, RILE, RICE, RICH. (100%)

March: The presents cost $30, $25, $20, and $40. (85%)

April: A minimum of three buses (90%)

May: SABER (or SABRE) and BEARS are the missing words. (90%)

June: Seven of each coin (84%)

July: Start at the upper left corner.

> HE SPOKE JUST ONCE.
> "LOOK, HANS, NO MA," HE SAID. (95%)

August: ATTENTIVE and TENTATIVE (65%)

September: Five (35%)

October: (30%)

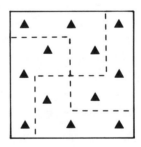

November: CONTROVERSY; SUPERNOVA; INNOVATIVE (95%)

December: Farmer Jones's fowl weighed 6 pounds each, and Farmer Smith's weighed 5 pounds each. (80%)

Day 7 of Each Month

January: The answer is FRUIT. (92%)

February: The correct answer is 4.8, not 5, miles per hour. The answer is obtained by dividing the distance covered by the time elapsed, and *any* distance will do. Take a 12-mile run, for instance. That will take them two hours out and three hours back. It therefore took them five hours to travel 24 miles. (60%)

March: CHEESE, FRUIT, and MEAT; APPLES, PEARS, and PLUMS (100%)

April: There are 301 tiles. This is the smallest number that will give you a remainder of 1 when divided by 2, 3, 4, 5, and 6, but divided by 7 leaves nothing over. (45%)

May: The lid weighs $6\frac{2}{3}$ ounces. (75%)

June: Maria was twenty-four. She subtracted one-seventh of her real age. (50%)

July: There are thirty-two three-legged animals and nineteen with two legs. (65%)

August: BANANA, PINEAPPLE, KIWI FRUIT, and PEACH; PIZZA, SPAGHETTI, and MEATBALLS; CAKE, PUDDING, and CREAM PUFFS (75%)

September: CHINA; SWEDEN; SPAIN (98%)

October: PARTING and PRATING (75%)

November: 1694 (85%)

December: EDISON CALLED. SAID HE COULD SHED SOME LIGHT ON THE SUBJECT. (90%)

Day 8 of Each Month

January: BIRDS OF A FEATHER FLOCK TOGETHER. (88%)

February: With the right answers you are left with MENSA. (85%)

March: AIRMEN, MARINE, and REMAIN. Ninety-five percent of the Mensans responded with all three words.

April: HAND (95%)

May: MAYONNAISE; AMAZINGLY. One hundred percent of the Mensa members answered this puzzle right, though some had trouble spelling MAYONNAISE.

June: D31. The sequence is made up of the initials of the months and the number of days in each month. (94%)

July: He saved 65.7 percent on fuel, using 34.3 percent of what he did before. (65%)

August: $42 (85%)

September: "T" is the missing letter, and the word is ANATHEMA. (75%)

October: FALL, HALL, HALE, HOLE, HOLD, COLD (98%)

November: THROW and WORTH; ROOST and TORSO; GAZER and GRAZE (98%)

December: MINUTE and MINUET will fill out the sentence. (100%)

Day 9 of Each Month

January: GIGGLING; HAMMERMAN; WILLOWWARE. Of Mensans who took this quiz, 92% got all three correct. A few more missed only one word.

February: (75%)

$$\begin{array}{r} 23 \\ 23 \\ 23 \\ \underline{23} \\ 92 \end{array}$$

March: There are fifty-five squares of all sizes in this design. Seventy percent of the Mensa members got this one right. Wrong answers ranged from twenty-six (all the small squares plus the large one) to 166.

April: Monday (100%)

May: The toys are priced at 7¢ per consonant, so a pinwheel costs 35¢. (45%)

June: SPRITE and STRIPE will fill out the sad story. (96%)

July: Jack won by one yard. He can run 100 yards while Jill can run 90, so with 10 yards left, the two of them are tied. (60%)

August: DOGGED; DOGMA; SEADOG (95%)

September: The answer to the problem is 0, once you multiply by the 0 on the telephone dial. Seventy-five percent of the Mensans who tried this puzzle said they did it within thirty seconds.

October: None of them could be Truthtellers. (35%)

November: BOSSES SOB; RENO LONER (70%)

December: DRAW, O COWARD; NO ROMAN A MORON (65%)

Day 10 of Each Month

January: 1349. Several Mensa members said they worked out this answer by logic. If the second number is three times the first, and the last is three times the second, then the last number must be 9. It's easy to work backward from there. (96%)

February: ALL THAT GLITTERS IS NOT GOLD. (100%)

March: Seven operators (65%)

April: Mensaman flew at 666.67 miles per hour over his entire trip. (90%)

May: Andy likes Byron. He only likes words whose first two letters make separate words: or, to, be, by. (35%)

June: Barbara likes jodhpurs because she only likes foreign words. Forty-five percent got the correct answer and the reason.

July: He makes it with more than 5 gallons to spare. (65%)

August: (35%)

$$\begin{array}{r} 927 \\ \underline{63} \\ 58401 \end{array}$$

September: CAL, BILL (also REA); HATTIE and SALLY; GEORGE and NORA (90%)

October: When no distinction is made between the hour and minute hands, the clock would look the same at 8:23 A.M., 4:42 P.M., and 8:23 P.M. (85%)

November: FOOLS RUSH IN WHERE ANGELS FEAR TO TREAD. (100%)

December: SNOW is the answer. (95%)

Day 11 of Each Month

January: $1.00. Wonkles cost 1¢ each, and winkles cost 2¢. (88%)

February: FEBRILE; INDEFENSIBLE; FEEBLE. All the Mensans figured out FEBRILE and FEEBLE, but only 45 percent found INDEFENSIBLE.

March: KNITTER (100%)

April: SMART (95%)

May: April is six, May is nine, and June is twenty. (55%)

June: JACK BE NIMBLE, JACK BE QUICK, FOR THE LIGHT JUST CHANGED AND THE ROAD IS SLICK. (65%)

July: LAPWING; PLOVER; GREBE; CARDINAL (90%)

August: HOW'S YOUR MOM, TOM? WELL, APPARENTLY. Start at the top left. (70%)

September: Thirty percent found this square, while 65 percent came up with other solutions, including one which used the word *neve,* a type of granular snow.

```
P  I  N  E
I  D  E  A
N  E  W  S
E  A  S  Y
```

October: The missing number is 120. (70%)

November: PERSHING, FOCH, and CHURCHILL; BASTOGNE, YPRES, and EL ALAMEIN (60%)

December: Their sons were ten and fifteen. (75%)

Day 12 of Each Month

January: CHEDDAR; ROQUEFORT; and LIMBURGER (100%)

February: You have twenty of each coin. (85%)

March: A bicycle costs $10.50 at this toy store. The owner charges $1.50 for each letter. (85%)

April: (50%)

$$\begin{array}{r} 715 \\ 46 \\ \hline 32890 \end{array}$$

May: The most common word square, turned in by 75 percent of the Mensans, was:

$$\begin{array}{cccc} O & G & R & E \\ G & O & A & L \\ R & A & T & S \\ E & L & S & E \end{array}$$

June: Half a dozen dozen, if you like dimes. That's six dozen, while a dozen and a half is eighteen. It's not just six of one and half a dozen of the other. (96%)

July: $51.20. You've marked it down 20 percent each time. One Mensa member told me he'd never buy a TV that was baroque! (75%)

August: PARSLEY, SARDINE, SAUSAGE, and BARLEY (75%)

September: KEEPSAKE, PERISCOPE, EDITED, and EMBLEM (65%)

October: COLUMBUS (70%)

November: There are ten youngsters, each received $5.00, and this puzzle contains a great deal of extraneous information. (90%)

December: D is the missing letter. The words are DRAIN, NADIR, DINAR, DIARY, DAIRY, PALED, PLEAD, and PEDAL, in no particular order. (65%)

Day 13 of Each Month

January: TEDIOUS and OUTSIDE are the missing words. (84%)

February: Jennifer is fifteen, in a system that awards five for each syllable. (75%)

March: Because the word *phobia* has Greek roots, you use Greek prefixes with it to make new words. AILUROPHOBIA (from the Greek *ailouros,* cat); XENOPHOBIA (from *xenos,* strange); and AGORAPHOBIA (from *agora,* open marketplace). (85%)

April: ACRES, CARES, RACES, and SCARE are the missing anagrams. (100%)

May: Eight. There were forty-eight states before Alaska, four winds blowing, forty thieves, and thirty-one days in May. (80%)

June: Cubes A and C cannot be made. This is a good test of your structural visualization skills. (75%)

July: "I LIKE THESE CHIPS," SAID TOM CRISPLY. Start with the middle letter in the top line. (90%)

August: DAWN, DARN, DARK, DIRK, DISK, DUSK is one route. (100%)

September: TRANSEPT; STEEPLEJACK; SEPARATE (100%)

October: Nine. Columbus sailed in 1492 with three ships in his fleet, and Mary married Henry VIII of England. (90%)

November: Sixty-six and forty-four (85%)

December: $5762.50 (85%)

Day 14 of Each Month

January: FAIL, PAIL, PALL, PALS, PASS. There were several variations on this pattern, but 100 percent of the Mensa members found one that worked.

February: The same hour and forty minutes (90%)

March: RAISE and RAZE, which mean "to erect" and "to tear down." There were other suggestions, such as WHOLE and HOLE, but this is the only pair of homonyms we found with exactly opposite meanings. (40%)

April: Answer (b), 104 96, fits the two series involved, one starting up from 101, the other starting down from 99. (90%)

May: There are two ways you can have fifty coins totalling $1.00: two dimes, forty pennies, and eight nickels; or two dimes, forty-five pennies, two nickels, and one quarter. These arrangements are equally probable, so there is a one-half chance you had a quarter to begin with. The probability that you then dropped that quarter from all the coins in your hand is one fiftieth. Therefore, the total probability that you lost a quarter is one half times one fiftieth, or one one-hundredth. (15%)

June: Our ages now are seventy-three and thirty-seven. (75%)

July: Pierre started with $64. He spent $34 for the Sauternes (a real bargain), $18 for the foie gras (also cheap), and $10 for the special brioche customarily eaten with this combination of foods. That left $2.00 for the inevitable medication for the liver—Americans have heartburn, but the French have crises of the liver. (90%)

August: INAUGURATE; DAUGHTER; HAUGHTY; LAUGHED (95%)

September: He has bills worth $50, $20, $10, $5.00, $2.00, and $1.00. Most people forget about the Thomas Jefferson two-dollar bill, but it's still out there. (75%)

October: My friend the test pilot was named Susan. (65%)

November: (95%)

December: Twenty-four pieces of gum (90%)

Day 15 of Each Month

January: The total for the top row of snowflakes is 91. (48%)

February: Samantha won. Just make a chart of all the information you have. (90%)

March: Seconds in 100 hours, by far: 360,000 seconds as against 3600 inches in 100 yards. (100%)

April: AN EFFICIENT BUSINESSWOMAN WHO FOUND A MACHINE THAT WOULD DO HALF HER WORK BOUGHT TWO. (90%)

May: "THERE IS NO WATER," SAID TOM DRYLY. (95%)

June: That she was lying. A Liar can't admit that he's a Liar, as she said she heard a man doing, because then he would be telling the truth about himself. The woman is either a Liar or, perhaps, an outsider like you. (85%)

July: RAIN is the missing word. July 15 is Saint Swithin's Day, and the story goes that if it rains on Saint Swithin's, it will rain for forty days thereafter. Conversely, if Saint Swithin's is dry, it will be fair for forty more days. Meteorological records don't bear out this tradition. (95%)

August: This puzzle was included in the belief that you wouldn't want to do anything more intellectually strenuous in August. (100%)

H	T	E	A
A	E	T	H
T	H	A	E
E	A	H	T

September: D is the missing letter. The words are DUNCE, CRUDE, DUCAT, CHARD, RADIO or DORIA, and DIVAN or VIAND. (75%)

October: There are several ways, but the most common was: A, RA, ARE, CARE, SCARE, CARESS, CASTERS. (90%)

November: He was Amy's brother-in-law—and the baby's uncle. (75%)

December: 13579 (80%)

Day 16 of Each Month

January: The answer I originally thought up was:

Twenty percent of Mensans replying to this question found that answer. But another 20 percent came up with:

Take your pick.

February: KALE, LAKE, and LEAK (100%)

March: MADDER; MARKETPLACE; MEAGER (100%)

April: $60 (70%)

May: SCARE is the oddity. All the other words are anagrams of each other. (90%)

June: She lives at number 1640. (20%)

July: Sally (35%)

August: The knight will arrive at 12:45. The Princess might do better with someone who knows he shouldn't just average speed and distance. (75%)

September: A is 1, B is 2, and so on up to J is 0. Then the puzzle works out to $(123456789 \times 9) + 10 = 1111111111$. (45%)

October: The new price will be \$102.90; the merchant reduced it 30 percent each time. (90%)

November: (80%)

$$
\begin{array}{cccc}
S & O & L & E \\
O & P & E & N \\
L & E & A & D \\
E & N & D & S \\
\end{array}
$$

December: Monday (95%)

Day 17 of Each Month

January: HE WHO IS TOO SHARP SOMETIMES CUTS HIMSELF. The code is the alphabet reversed, so that Z becomes A, Y becomes B, and so on. (84%)

February: You made \$15. Only 75 percent of the Mensa members got this one. Their most common error was not realizing that you have to treat each transaction separately. Then simply add up all the money laid out and all the money taken in. The fact that you bought the same lamp twice is irrelevant.

March:

E	I	N	R
N	R	E	I
R	N	I	E
I	E	R	N

This was the most common solution, though there are at least two more. (90%)

April: 26789 (95%)

May: Will power: admirable in ourselves but plain stubbornness when we find it elsewhere (55%)

June: Eve called. Apple season over. Will peaches be OK? (65%)

July: 16. The middle figure is derived by adding the numbers in the surrounding circles and squaring the result. (80%)

August: It is much too hot to do these things right now! The key is one to the left on a Qwerty typewriter. More relief from the August heat. (95%)

September: The only thing worse than not getting what you want is getting what you want. (85%)

October: 5931 (95%)

November: Glow, slow, slot, soot, foot, fort, form, worm. Other solutions used food and ford. (95%)

December: Jim's daughter is only six months old, and Jim is thirty and a half years old. If the baby were one year, Jim would have to be thirty, which is only twenty-nine years older. (75%)

Day 18 of Each Month

January: Only 62 percent of the Mensans got all four examples correct, but 98 percent found two or more.

193	175	195	295
275	293	273	173
468	468	468	468

February: Mother, Mom, or whatever he called his mother (95%)

March: He is your father. (90%)

April: The bride was thirty, the groom twenty-seven. (55%)

May: He had twenty minutes. (50%)
The puzzles for May 17 and 18 marked a clear division between Mensans who are verbally inclined and those who are mathematically inclined. Those who succeeded with May 17 (55%) tended to get May 18 wrong (50%), and vice versa.

June: A plum is worth 4¢. The proprietor values one penny per letter, with any letter in a pair counted twice. (55%)

July: Twenty pounds (82%)

August: MANE, MEAN, AMEN, and NAME (95%)

September: DIRT, DINT, DENT, LENT, LEND, LEAD, LOAD, ROAD is the most common solution. (95%)

October: Sally (75%)

November: CLEVER (80%)

December: Two tosses of the 16-point ring and four tosses of the 17-point ring. Your aim is perfect, of course. (85%)

Day 19 of Each Month

January: BRAID and RABID are the only two commonly accepted anagrams. (96%)

February: A COMMITTEE IS A GROUP THAT KEEPS MINUTES BUT WASTES HOURS. (65%)

March: FISSURE and FUSSIER; SUPREME and PRESUME; PRESENT, REPENTS, and SERPENT. (90%)

April: Twenty people split a $600 bill. (65%)

May: $20 (75%)

June: If you and your friend each have ten coins totaling 49¢, then they must be four pennies, three dimes, and three nickels. Between you, you have six dimes out of twenty coins. The chance is six out of twenty, or 30 percent. (65%)

July: The clock will be five minutes fast at sunset on the twenty-eighth day. Of course, it will lose time and become more correct during the night that follows, so it won't be five minutes fast at sunrise until the thirtieth day. Seventy-five percent of the Mensa members realized that the twenty-eighth day was correct, and one-third of those noted that the thirtieth day was also significant.

August: You can form the word COLD in twelve ways, though it won't make you any colder. (55%)

September: (90%)

```
L  I  K  E
I  D  E  A
K  E  P  T
E  A  T  S
```

October: The cleverest answer seems to be SCHEYE: SCH as in schism, and EYE as in eye. (95%)

November: Fifteen of each coin (90%)

December: GRASS, CRASS, CRESS, CREES, CREED, GREED, GREEN (95%)

Day 20 of Each Month

January: You can't do it at all. For example, if your run is 6 miles, you would have to do it in one hour to average 6 miles per hour. However, you've already taken an hour to do the first half of the run, thereby using all the available time. (30%)

February: LUXEMBOURG, HUNGARY, and ARGENTINA (90%)

March: Sheree had $1.80 in play money, and Tyler had $1.40 (75%).

April: There were a good many answers that didn't fit the puzzle's criteria, such as PA, PAS, PASS, which uses slang. Only 25 percent of the Mensa members came up with good English words. CARE, CARES, CARESS was one common set; PRINCE, PRINCES, PRINCESS was another; and there are probably more.

May: THE ONLY DATA TO PROVE ME RIGHT / ARE THOSE I DID NOT SAVE. Start at the upper left corner. (60%)

June: Cristoforo was Isabella's grandfather and Ferdinand's grandfather-in-law. (95%)

July: JULIET; JONQUIL; JUBILANT (98%)

August: 20 (85%)

September: The word is MAR. (70%)

October: 161 large and 224 small sacks (70%)

November: Sally likes cheese because it has a double letter. (95%)

December: 108 (95%)

Day 21 of Each Month

January: Jim was last. Just set up a chart of the runners. (100%)

February: The probability is 85 percent. There are only two ways in which fifty coins can total $1.00. One is forty-five pennies, two nickels, two dimes, and a quarter; the other is forty pennies, eight nickels, and two dimes. So there are eighty-five chances out of one hundred that the coin was a penny. (30%)

March: Six salesmen can sell sixty stoves in seventy minutes. (65%)

April: The missing letter is S. If you spiral clockwise around each square into the center, and then move on to the next square, you spell out THIS PUZZLE IS MADE OF SQUARES. (40%)

May: PORTFOLIO; PERSEVERE or PRESERVE (35%)

June: METHYLENE; DUNDERHEAD; DISSENSION (44%)

July: REPAPER; TUBE DEBUT (75%)

August: MONEY TALKS, BUT TO ME IT SAYS GOODBYE. Just substitute letters for their numerical place in the alphabet. (65%)

September: FALL (100%)

October: WAS IT A CAR OR A CAT I SAW? (75%) NOT NEW YORK, ROY WENT ON. (65%)

November: Sixty-four (75%)

December: You have a paradox. No one who lies all the time can say he is a Liar. Therefore the man is not a Liar, though he is lying. You are outside Liars and Truthtellers Town at last. Forty-five percent of the Mensa members spotted the paradox.

Day 22 of Each Month

January: You have twenty-four coins of each kind. (92%)

February: ROOSEVELT, TRUMAN, and KENNEDY; JOHNSON, TYLER, and JEFFERSON; TAFT, COOLIDGE, and WASHINGTON (100%)

March: Two pounds 4 ounces (or $2\frac{1}{4}$ pounds or 36 ounces). Three-fourths of three-fourths of a pound is 9 ounces, so the fish weighed 9 ounces plus the remaining three-fourths of its weight. Or, 9 ounces is one-quarter of its weight. (55%)

April: If you have good geographical knowledge, you found the word CORRECT after crossing out letters. (70%)

May: MADAME CURIE CALLED. SAID SHE WAS GETTING GLOWING REPORTS ON HER WORK. The substitution is the alphabet numbered backward. (90%)

June: Six of each coin. (95%)

July: Thirteen triangles (85%)

August: Abe had seven pennies and Lizzy thirteen. (75%)

September: There were six students. (90%)

October: Seventy-five percent of the Mensa members found at least one anti-magic square. Here's an example:

3	4	5
2	1	6
9	8	7

November: She said, "No." Furthermore, you know she is a Liar and her companion is a Truthteller. If they were both Liars, both Truthtellers, or she was a Truthteller and her companion a Liar, she would have answered, "Yes"—and you wouldn't have known whether she was lying. (45%)

December: No, you can't solve it. For topographical reasons, you will always miss one line segment. But there are some very creative ways to cheat!

Day 23 of Each Month

January: MANILA; SCHUBERT; PASTEUR; NAPLES. VIKING cannot be anagrammed. Eighty-eight percent of the Mensans got this right; the name missed most was SCHUBERT.

February: Of the twelve pies, Sally must have brought three, Jane four, and Hector five. Dividing the meal evenly, they ate three pies apiece. That means William paid $3.00. Sally ate the three pies she brought (or their equivalent). Jane, who brought four, got $1.00 for the extra pie she contributed, and Hector, who brought five pies got $2.00. (45%)

March: RECIPE and PIERCE (95%)

April: CONSIDERATION (90%)

May: (65%)

$$
\begin{array}{r}
7142 \\
7142 \\
\underline{7142} \\
21426
\end{array}
$$

June: ADJUNCT; JUVENILE; JUNIPER; JOURNAL (95%)

July: Sally was short by 6.75 inches. She needed 180 inches, but the owner gave her only 165 plus 5 percent of that. (60%)

August: THE ONLY THING WORSE THAN A HUSBAND WHO NEVER NOTICES WHAT YOU COOK OR WHAT YOU WEAR IS A HUSBAND WHO ALWAYS NOTICES WHAT YOU COOK AND WHAT YOU WEAR. (90%)

September: CONNIVER (100%)

October: Tom was twenty, Professor Jones sixty-four. (65%)

November: $35.30 and $29.85 (75%)

December: Because my red-haired colleague is male.

Day 24 of Each Month

January: ATE FETA; ELBA TABLE. Sixty percent had both right, and 80 percent had one (usually ELBA TABLE) right.

February: ANGEL, ANGLE, and GLEAN (100%)

March: BRAIN (75%)

April: TOO MANY BOOKS SPOIL THE CLOTH. Start at the upper left corner. (90%)

May: CHEER (95%)

June: This puzzle caused major problems when two eminent mathematicians came up with alternate answers! One had pairs of weights at 1, 4, 24, and 55 pounds. The other insisted equally vehemently that the weights were 1, 4, 16, and 64 pounds. Who was right? They both are! Only 40 percent of the Mensa members did this puzzle, and they split their votes between the two answers.

July: I'd save four hours, not counting recovery time. (90%)

August: PORTUGAL; DENMARK; ZAIRE (75%)

September: PLASTER and STAPLER (75%)

October: "Z" is the missing letter; the words are, clockwise from the top, WOOZY, GLAZE, LAZED, HAZEL, BRAZE, RAZES, DOZEN, and ZONED. (90%)

November: FIRST WE STUFF THE TURKEY; AND THEN WE STUFF OURSELVES. (90%)

December: My friend is too short to reach the button in the elevator for the fifteenth floor—he can reach only as high as ten. On the way down, the first-floor button is easy for him to reach.

Day 25 of Each Month

January: CHINA; CANADA; PERU (100%)

February: DEB ABED; DELIA AND EDNA AILED. (95%)

March: It's now 1:00 A.M. (100%)

April: (40%)

$$
\begin{array}{r}
757 \\
757 \\
45 \\
\hline
1559
\end{array}
$$

May: Six. Each seamstress sews one seam in twenty minutes. (75%)

June: WETTISH and WHITEST are the only common English words Mensans could find. (90%)

July: ADMIRER and MARRIED (25%)

August: COURTS, because all the others are anagrams of each other (90%)

September: People who live in grass houses shouldn't stow thrones. (95%)

October: There were seven of them. (80%)

November: The watchman had been sleeping on the job. Otherwise, he wouldn't have been dreaming. (80%)

December: One hundred fifty minutes *is* two and a half hours.

Day 26 of Each Month

January: Each little bag of chocolates cost 3¢. (80%)

February: PERMEATE, REHEARSE, TEENAGER, FORESEER (65%)

March: CATAMARAN, CALAMARI, and MARCHIONESS (90%)

April: The next day, or tomorrow (95%)

May: The missing letter is "Y." Clockwise from the top the words are: GUSHY, JOLLY, YAWED, WEARY, OXEYE, and YOUNG. (25%)

June: POLAND, CANADA, and INDIA are hidden in these sentences. (95%)

July: ABSTEMIOUS(LY), AERONAUTICS, FACETIOUS(LY), NEFARIOUS, PNEUMONIA, and SEQUOIA are the most common. One hundred percent of the Mensans polled thought of at least three, but only 40 percent found six.

August: ABSTEMIOUSLY; Sallie Lou likes to have all five vowels in her words. Some of her other favorites are listed in the July 26 answer above. (70%)

September: $81, left from an original $100 (75%)

October: $100 (90%)

November: You've lost 2 gallons, or 50 miles' worth of driving. Seventy percent of the Mensans got this right as far as the math was concerned, and there were some interesting but unprintable suggestions about what they'd say to the dealer who sold them that nice new car.

December: The oldest boy asked Daddy for another dollar, making $18. He took $9.00, gave the middle brother $6.00, and gave the baby $2.00. Then he returned the extra dollar to Daddy.

Day 27 of Each Month

January: "THE TIME HAS COME," THE WALRUS SAID, / "TO TALK OF MANY THINGS: / OF SHOES—AND SHIPS—AND SEALING-WAX— / OF CABBAGES—AND KINGS." These immortal lines and many others came from the pen of Charles Dodgson. He achieved worldwide fame as children's author Lewis Carroll, but not as the logician he really was. There is a perhaps apocryphal story that Queen Victoria so enjoyed his *Through the Looking-Glass* that she asked him, as a favor, to send her his next book. Shortly thereafter, she received an abstruse mathematical text. She was not amused. (75%)

February: Because $6 = 3 \times 2$, then $6 \times 5 = (3 \times 2) \times 5 = 3 \times (2 \times 5)$. If "twice 5 is 9," according to the conditions of the problem, the answer is $3 \times 9 = 27$. This type of puzzle is often used to introduce students to the idea of base numbers other than 10. (80%)

March: PERSISTING is the only word we can find, and only 60 percent of the Mensans found it.

April: Dot likes a star. She only likes words that also spell words backward. (90%)

May: You had fifteen eggs to begin with. (85%)

June: Darlene likes 1600. She only likes perfect squares. (65%)

July: Fifty-seven. The forty-nine recycled from the original batch could be recycled themselves, and so on. (44%)

August: $16 (75%)

September: The trains are 40 miles apart. (85%)

October: Sheila had fifty-eight favors and planned to buy two more. (60%)

November: "WE'RE UNDER THE CHURCH," SAID TOM CRYPTICALLY. Start at the top left. (75%)

December: When we meet, we're the same distance from Boston.

Day 28 of Each Month

January: A ROAD MAP TELLS YOU EVERYTHING EXCEPT HOW TO REFOLD IT. You start at the A in the middle of the array. (84%)

February: 2688 (100%)

March: COLD, CORD, WORD, WARD, WARM. One hundred percent of the Mensans who did this puzzle found either this solution or one which used WOLD.

April: (75%)

```
4  1  4
1     1
4  1  4
```

May: Yourself (90%)

June: If you want to be absolutely certain, you have to pick out eleven pieces of fruit. Your first ten might be five nectarines and five peaches, unlikely as that is. (95%)

July: There were several answers, but the square that 65 percent of the Mensans found was:

```
H  A  B  I  T
A  R  O  S  E
B  O  I  L  S
I  S  L  E  T
T  E  S  T  S
```

August: Jack is forty-seven, and John is forty-one. (75%)

September: The older one got 55¢, and the younger got 30¢. (95%)

October: WITCH (95%)

November: 1, 2, and 3 (90%)

December: Your aged grandmother is pulling your leg. Nineteen hundred was not a Leap Year under the Gregorian calendar since it was not divisible by 400. But the year 2000 will be.

Day 29 of Each Month

January: SMART (90%)

February: Colonel Cholomondely-Snaithworth-Jones was lying, and the explorers knew it. There are no wild tigers at the headwaters of the Nile, or anywhere else in Africa. Liars like the colonel come along only once every four years. (95%)

March: The missing letter is A. The words are, reading clockwise from the two on top, AMPLE, MAPLE, AILED, IDEAL, DOGMA, DWARF, DAFFY, and LAXLY. Sixty-five percent of the Mensa members found these words, with LAXLY giving the most trouble.

April: APRICOT; CAPTURED; CAPRICORN (95%)

May: The correct response is (b), S G. The series are the alphabet forward from A, skipping two letters, and the alphabet backward from Y, skipping two letters. (90%)

June: BANALITIES (75%)

July: Friday (90%)

August: WARD, KEY, LOCK, and MILL are the four words. (95%)

September: They chewed twenty-four pieces. (60%)

October: Of the 90 percent who did this puzzle correctly, 50 percent came up with this solution.

```
M  A  N  E
A  M  E  N
N  E  E  D
E  N  D  S
```

November: DYNAMO; AWKWARD; SYZYGY. The most commonly missed word was SYZYGY, an astronomical conjunction. (75%)

December: There are twenty 9's, the first in 9 and the last two in 99.

Day 30 of Each Month

January: Boxes A and D cannot be made from the unfolded box. A whopping 96 percent of the Mensa members answered this correctly; perhaps they cut out and folded the box.

March: No matter how many socks of a particular color there are, there are four different colors in the drawer. Your brother must take out five socks, or one more than there are colors, before he can be guaranteed a matching pair. (100%)

April: Maura started with $20. You work backward on these puzzles, starting with the fact that if half of what she has left plus $1.00 is all that she has, she must have $2.00 left. (65%)

May: There is no "E" at all in the paragraph. That's very uncommon, as "E" is the letter most used in English. (75%)

June: Bouquet, bridesmaid, and veil; groom, ring, and honeymoon; mother-in-law, flower girl, and wedding march (95%)

July: For exactly 50¢, you can buy seven peanut butter cups and one chocolate bar. If you're a bargain hunter, you can also buy eight peanut butter cups for only 48¢. (50%)

August: 12643 (65%)

September: (85%)

0	12	12	0
8	4	4	8
4	8	8	4
12	0	0	12

October: One sister was allowed to cut the cake in two, and the other got first choice of the two pieces. (75%)

November: 4:00 P.M. (65%)

December: The amateur was swindled. No authentic coins are dated B.C., because no one knew then that the era would eventually be called B.C. In fact, "before" is an English word, and English hadn't been developed.

Day 31 of Each Month

January: Jacinth; janissary; Jeffersonian (85%) (Many missed janissary.)

March: Tony likes tomatoes. He only likes words that start with prepositions. (65%)

May: MA IS AS SELFLESS AS I AM; RED RUM, SIR, IS MURDER. Ninety percent found the second palindrome, but only 30 percent solved the first.

July: (45%)

$$\begin{array}{r} 402 \\ 39 \\ \hline 15678 \end{array}$$

August: IT IS VERY HARD TO WIN AN ARGUMENT WHEN THE OTHER SIDE ISN'T BOTHERED BY TELLING UNTRUTHS. (35%)

October: There are four witches and twelve cats. (80%)

December: Joe was speaking on December 31, his birthday. He was twenty on December 30, turned twenty-one on December 31, and will be twenty-two next year on December 31. This puzzle was tested on a ninety-year-old woman neighbor, who saw it immediately.

How to Join Mensa

Now that you've read about Mensa and matched wits with Mensa members, why don't you write to:

American Mensa, Ltd.
Dept. AT
2626 East 14th Street
Brooklyn, NY   11235–3992

In Canada, write to:

Canadian Mensa, Dept. W
P.O. Box 505, Station S
Toronto, Ontario   M5M 4L8

You will receive information about how to take a standard intelligence test, or what tests you may already have taken might qualify you for membership. A score at the ninety-eighth percentile (the top 2 percent of the population) is the only requirement for joining Mensa. Information on the Mensa scholarships, funded in part by the sale of this book, is also available from American Mensa Ltd.